What Brain Research Says about Student Learning

What Brain Research Says about Student Learning

How Parents and Teachers Can Capitalize on It for Student Success

Perry R. Rettig and Toni M. Bailey

ROWMAN & LITTLEFIELD
Lanham • Boulder • New York • London

Published by Rowman & Littlefield
An imprint of The Rowman & Littlefield Publishing Group, Inc.
4501 Forbes Boulevard, Suite 200, Lanham, Maryland 20706
www.rowman.com

86-90 Paul Street, London EC2A 4NE

Copyright © 2024 by Perry R. Rettig, Toni M. Bailey

All rights reserved. No part of this book may be reproduced in any form or by any electronic or mechanical means, including information storage and retrieval systems, without written permission from the publisher, except by a reviewer who may quote passages in a review.

British Library Cataloguing in Publication Information Available

Library of Congress Cataloging-in-Publication Data Available

ISBN 978-1-4758-7207-1 (cloth)
ISBN 978-1-4758-7208-8 (pbk.)
ISBN 978-1-4758-7209-5 (ebook)

Contents

Dedication	vii
Preface	ix
Introduction	1
Part I: The Brain	15
Part II: Learning Theory	53
Part III: Implications and Applications	73
Annotated Bibliography	105
Bibliography	109
About the Authors	115

Dedication

This book has been years in the making. It took a professional lifetime of teaching experience, for the both of us, to research and write. As such, we have received a lifetime of support from our loved ones. This book is dedicated to our children.

Kelly Rettig Paulsen and Lisa Rettig Neely have been tremendous influencers. At every step along the way, Perry has asked, "How does this knowledge and these concepts impact Lisa and Kelly and how they raise their four sons?" As wonderfully dedicated parents, they strive to work with their children's teachers and at home to provide the greatest impact on the futures of their boys.

Zion and Sinai Bailey, Toni's little heartbeats, have upheld their duties of constantly reminding her how intricate and robust the child's mind truly is. They are waves of energy, absorbing everything in their environment and teaching their mom how they learn along the way.

Of course, this book is dedicated to all those current and future teachers and parents who strive on a daily basis to provide the best learning experience possible for our children. You are charged with the amazing responsibility of providing the citizens of tomorrow with efficient skillsets for the sake of furthering our society. Therefore, an understanding of how individuals learn, both theoretically and practically, is a critical need. We dedicate this book to your dedication—your triumphs and struggles, and your professional ethos in whatever your content area. All our students benefit from your dedication, professionalism, and ethic.

Preface

What Brain Research Says about Student Learning: How Parents and Teachers can Capitalize on It for Student Success is written by life-long educators for parents and teachers of PK–12 students. We have worked in both PK–12 and higher education settings our entire careers. Among other topics, we teach undergraduate and graduate courses entitled "Learning and Cognition," designed for school teachers and leaders. It is from these perspectives we share our experiences and insights.

"'Learn' is an active verb"; according to the National Academies of Sciences, Engineering, and Medicine:

> It is something people do, not something that happens to them. People are not passive recipients of learning. . . . Instead, through acting in the world, people encounter situations, problems, and ideas. By engaging with these situations, problems, and ideas, they have social, emotional, cognitive, and physical experiences, and they adapt.[1]

While teachers are steeped in learning theory, new insights about how the brain learns, develops, comprehends, and makes decisions can have dramatic impact in their classrooms and their understanding of learning models. Likewise, our experience as parents and educators shows that parents want to know more about how their children learn and how they themselves can work in tandem with their children's teachers. The aim of this book is to share insights about the brain and of the learning theories that educators use to inform their pedagogy.

The capacity for learning is essentially a never-ending process.[2] "It is usually risky to make generalizations about behavior based solely on age."[3] Children continuously experience events in their lives that they learn from and adapt their learning strategies over time. Learning is a developmental process. At various points in all our lives, we take on a variety of passive and active learner roles as we negotiate and navigate different learning situations. This book is written not from a largely technical and jargon-filled standpoint, but rather through the lens of real-life parents and practitioners in a very approachable fashion.

We will share insights from the fields of brain research and learning theory and then provide examples from our own experiences. Educators often refer to three levels of learning reflection: the What, the So What, and the Now What? The What is the actual knowledge or skills that we teach our students—it's "the stuff" of content. The So What is the general implications of what the students have learned in the classroom. The Now What is the actual application and higher-order thinking of what the students have learned in the classroom and are able to do.

Moving from content to application is the intent of this book. Our ultimate aim, then, is to help parents and teachers to reflect upon how their students learn and how to best support their learning. While we each may play different roles, working in tandem we can make a significant difference to our children's academic success. We can take What our children learn, and help them truly understand what they have learned—so they understand the So What? From there, we can make learning meaningful and applicable to life—the Now What?

As such, with new understanding about brain research and learning theory, teachers can examine their classroom environments, how they construct their lessons and the assignments they give, and how they assess their students' learning as well as the effectiveness of their own instruction. Parents can learn how to structure their home environment to support their children's school experience and have a much better understanding of their teachers' pedagogy.

It is our hope this book becomes a starting point for individual and group reflection. Faculty members can begin to have conversations around these topics and enjoin parents in these conversations. Parent-teacher organizations could serve as the perfect place for such meaningful dialogue to begin. Parents and teachers can join one another in discovering how they can work together to help our children succeed.

Finally, if you are a parent or a teacher of college-aged or adult students, we invite you to read our most recent book, *Brain Research and Learning Theory: Implications to Improve Student Learning and Engagement*. It is written in a very similar format for the target audience of college professors for college students.

NOTES

1. National Academies of Sciences, Engineering, and Medicine, *How People Learn II: Learners, Contexts, and Cultures* (Washington, DC: The National Academies Press, 2018), 12. The authors go on to indicate: "Many kinds of learning are promoted when the learner engages actively rather than passively, by developing her own models, for example, or deliberately developing a habit or modeling an observed behavior" (67).

2. Geraldine Holmes and Michele Abington-Cooper, "Pedagogy vs. Andragogy: A False Dichotomy," *Journal of Technology Studies* 26, 2 (2000), para 3.

3. Holmes and Abington-Cooper, "Pedagogy vs. Andragogy," para. 3.

Introduction

What Brain Research Says about Student Learning is written in a very straightforward manner. It is designed for parents and teachers to work together as partners to help their children learn. The first two parts of this book provide the framework and structure necessary to create an optimal learning environment—a culture, if you will, an informed pedagogy, and how assignments can expand students' understanding of the content. How student learning is assessed, and the effectiveness of instruction are also included.

It is the final part of the book, part III, which brings it all together by first describing implications for both the classroom instructor and the parent. It concludes with application—utilizing case studies to introduce real-life learning scenarios. These case studies were crafted to encompass a variety of perspectives, allowing readers to engage with diverse parent-student-teacher situations and providing practical examples that guide the reader's practice in applying the principles discussed throughout the book.

All K–12 educators have Bloom's Learning Taxonomy and Maslow's Hierarchy of Needs committed to memory. Both Abraham Maslow and Benjamin Bloom created models to help educators understand how people are motivated to learn and achieve, and the different levels of learning, respectively.

Maslow's Hierarchy of Needs clearly depicts the levels of people's motivation from the most basic to the most advanced (see figure I.1). Implications for the classroom setting and for pedagogy are enormous. The onus for motivation moves more from the adult to the student the higher one moves up the hierarchy.

Maslow's pyramid model contends that individual people are motivated by an ever-increasing hierarchy of needs. Starting at the bottom of the pyramid, people are motivated to take care of their most basic physiological needs, for example food and water. Once these needs are sufficiently met, the next level people seek is their own safety and security. If the individual's most basic

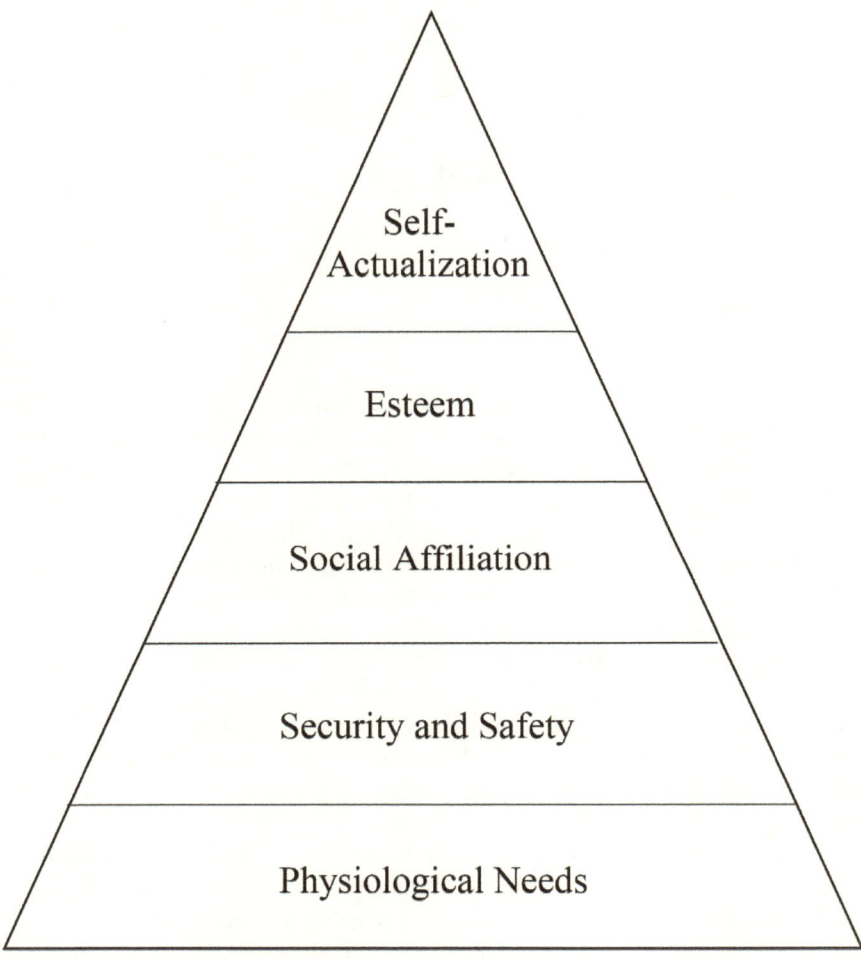

Figure I.1 Maslow's Hierarchy of Needs

needs are met and they feel safe, they are then motivated by a sense of love, belonging, and acceptance by others.

Once these lower-level needs are met, people are motivated by esteem and then ultimately by self-actualization. The former is a sense of self-esteem and recognition by peers. The final level includes a sense of becoming whole, having personal autonomy, and self-direction. As the model suggests, each of us strives to move higher up the pyramid and are typically not satisfied by the primary levels. Often, adults help fulfill the lower-level needs of youth, but the upper levels require more self-efficacy.

Hastings and West expressed the need for students to take ownership of their own learning because it provides direction and focus for their learning. In other words, students are motivated to actively achieve goals that they establish for themselves, to put forth the energy in the attainment of those goals and to persevere when obstacles are in the way.[1]

One can, however, slip back down the motivation pyramid at any time. For example, should a family's house be destroyed in a fire, they could slip from esteem needs to physiological needs. Similarly, a highly self-motivated professional might be given very unique and demanding new job responsibilities and subsequently slip down the hierarchy in the short term until they regain confidence and expertise. An example many teachers have experienced is moving from teaching face-to-face with content they have mastered to now teaching online.

Unknown to most educators, Maslow had begun work on a more elaborate model, but his work was never published because of his untimely death. However, figure I.2 highlights these enhanced levels.

Maslow's final, albeit unpublished, model expanded to include cognitive, aesthetic, and transcendence levels of needs. The former two are immediately after esteem and just prior to self-actualization. Transcendence had now usurped self-actualization as the penultimate level.

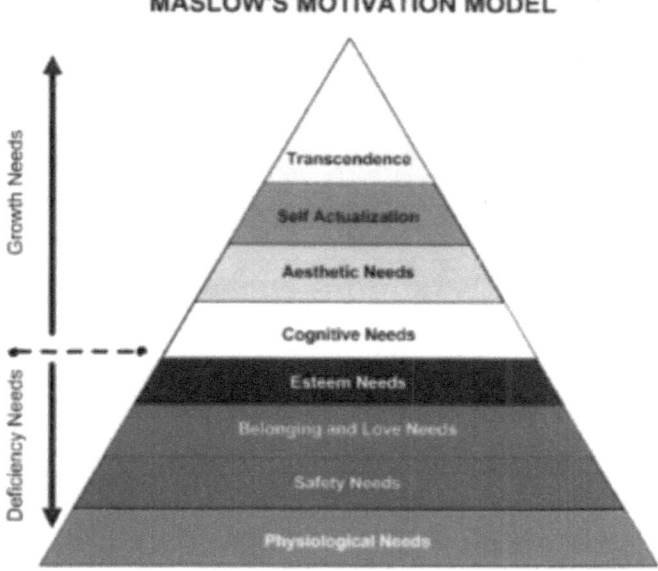

Figure I.2 Maslow's Unpublished Elaborated Hierarchy of Needs *Source:* Saul McLeod, "Maslow's Hierarchy of Needs," Simply Psychology, May 21, 2018), https//:www.simplypsychology.org/maslow.html

People are most motivated and compelled to transcend in life through their values to be interconnected with nature and with others. This is where an individual can get the most out of themselves and the most out of their organizations—when they relate and connect with one another to meet common goals and mission. It is not a selfish self-actualization—it is beyond that. It is transcendent self-actualization with the whole.

Other derivative versions of Maslow's Hierarchy of Needs have subsequently been created, mostly as they relate to the work environment, but for the sake of pedagogical discussion Maslow's original hierarchy remains prescient. This work will be discussed and explicated at length in part III.

On the other hand, Benjamin Bloom focused his conceptual research on levels of learning, from the most basic to the most advanced. All too often, much of what is taught and assessed in today's classrooms would be considered lower-level Bloom. The lower levels are critical and foundational learning, but they are far from sufficient. Further, many standardized and IQ tests focus at the lower levels on Bloom's learning taxonomy. The best teachers teach across the learning spectrum.

Scholars can't even agree how to define "intelligence." Educators are familiar with Howard Gardner's nine Multiple Intelligences: linguistic, logical or mathematical, visual or spatial, bodily or kinesthetic, musical, interpersonal, intrapersonal, naturalistic, and metaphysical.[2] Daniel Goleman's EQ or Emotional Intelligence[3] has received great publicity. Robert Sternberg identified three primary forms of intelligence in his Triarchic Model: analytic, creative, and practical.[4] These variety of models could be scattered across Bloom's spectrum but also would seem to show how difficult it is to measure IQ.

Bloom and his colleagues published his cognitive learning taxonomy in 1956.[5] This taxonomy has been reimagined[6] and derivatives[7] have been created over the years, but it remains the foundation of many good instructors' lesson planning. The original version was considered a more static list of objectives while newer versions are more dynamic and help to describe what learners actually do (see figure I.4).

As this book progresses, one might find that while learning is not linear, perhaps the taxonomy need not be viewed as such either. As learning is dynamic and integrated across domains, so too should the taxonomy be considered dynamic and integrated. An organic or circular depiction may serve as a better visualization (see figure I.5).

The lowest level of the revised Bloom's Taxonomy (see figure I.4) is remember, or the recalling of basic facts and concepts. This is followed by the higher level of understand, or to explain ideas and concepts. The next level is apply, or to use information in new situations, followed by analyze, or to draw connections among ideas. In the revised taxonomy, evaluate is now the next

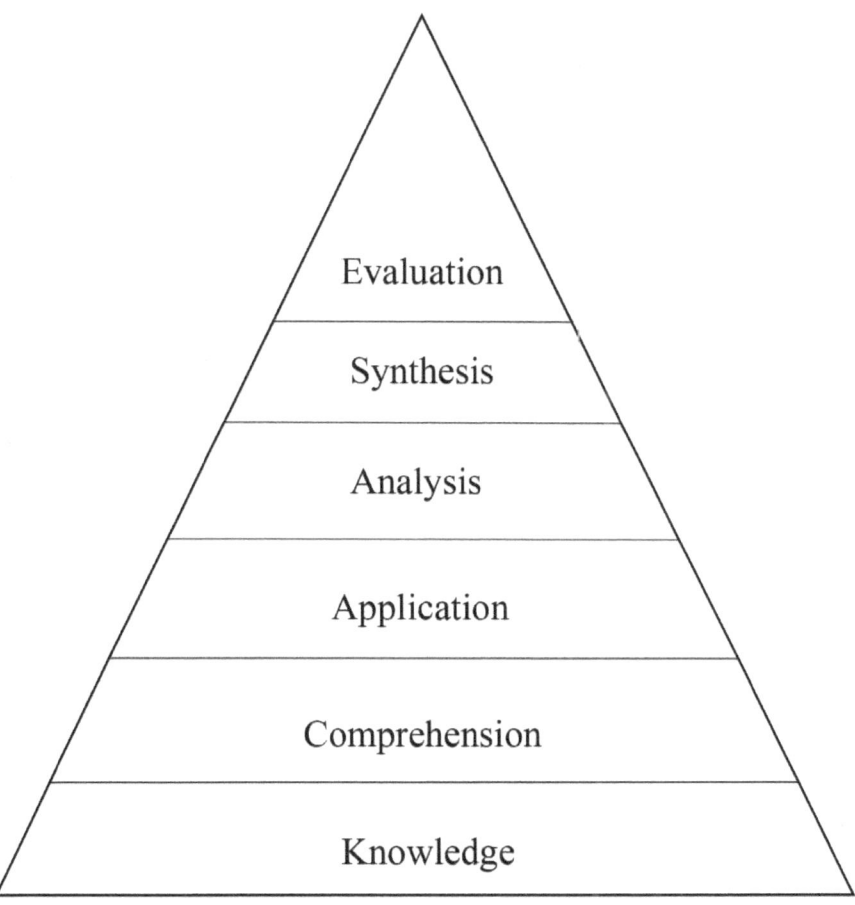

Figure I.3 Bloom's Original Learning Taxonomy

level where students justify a position or decision. The highest level is create, where the student is expected to produce new or original work.

Again, the implications of this model can be profound with respect to where teachers and parents focus their time and attention, what they expect of their learners, how they teach them, what assignments they give, and how they assess what the students have learned.

This seminal theoretical work provides the baseline for *What Brain Research Says about Student Learning*. Part I is devoted entirely to brain research—what is known about how the brain works in terms of taking in information, incorporating memories, and how it analyzes, synthesizes, organizes, evaluates, and creates. These understandings directly impact how teachers teach their content, the classroom environment they create, the kinds

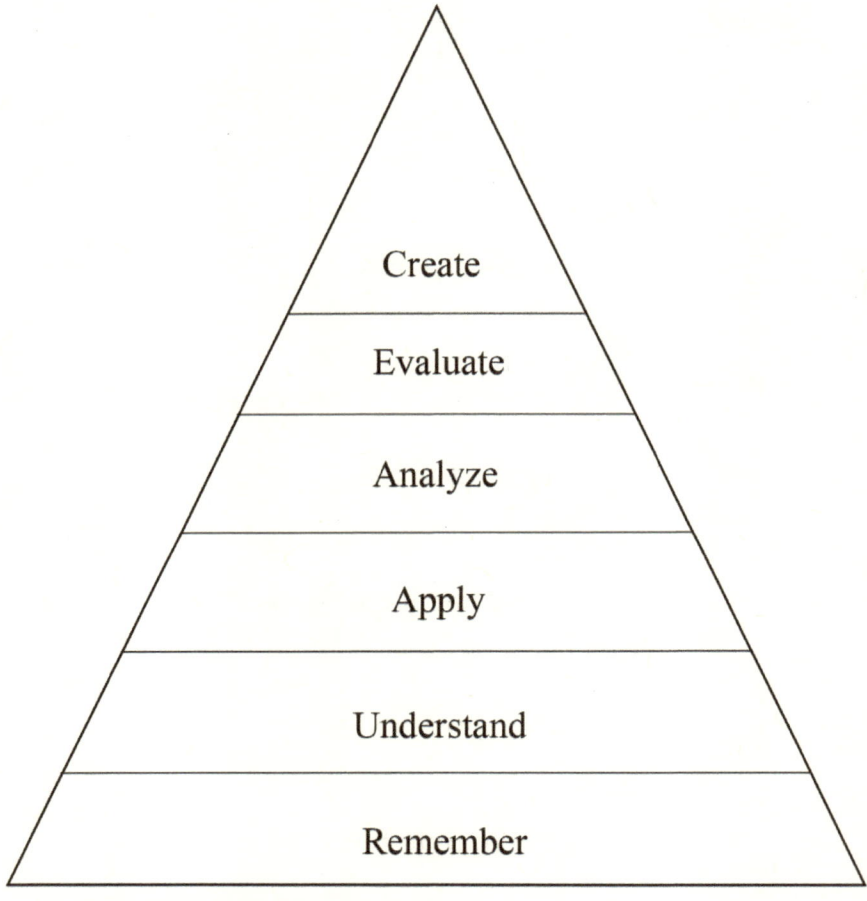

Figure I.4 Bloom's Revised Learning Taxonomy

of assignments they give, and how they assess their students' learning and the effectiveness of their own teaching.

For example, "the brain is poorly designed for formal instruction,"[8] at least in the way many instructors teach today. Learning is not isolated to one region; the learning process is diffuse across the brain. Also, a student's attention span is roughly one minute for every year of age. In other words, a ten-year-old has the attention span of ten minutes to focus on the learning at hand.

Students are motivated the most by work they find relevant, meaningful, and relatable to their own experiences—something not often found in many classrooms. One example of the paradox concerning traditional classroom planning is that the work-world students will enter is computer driven and

Figure I.5 Circular Model of Bloom's Taxonomy *Source:* Created by Dr. Toni Bailey

production-oriented, but today's classrooms are too often driven by paper and pencil and too exam-oriented.

"Intelligence is plastic and modifiable. All of our experiences result in the formation of neuronal circuits. The richer, more varied, and more challenging the experiences, the more elaborate the neuronal circuits,"[9] according to Richard Restak. Using only one mode for teaching misses the mark for many students, because the orthodox model of learning is often teacher-centered and based on authoritarian principles, and it leaves out numerous opportunities for better integration.

In expressing frustration with her own early teaching experiences, Laurie Materna quipped:

> You could say that these students were a captive audience in the traditional instructional paradigm, where teachers primarily used the didactic lecture method of disseminating volumes of information to large numbers of students. There was certainly a disparity between the learning style of the students and

the teaching style of most of the instructors. . . . I knew there had to be a better way to reach these students.[10]

On the other hand, according to Robert Sylwester:

Imaginative teachers have always used multiple approaches to the curriculum in order to open as many cognitive doors as possible. They presented information to students via one intelligence and then challenged them to paraphrase it using another. They developed open-ended projects that encouraged students to explore multiple approaches to the problem. They encouraged students with different interests and abilities to work together.[11]

With respect to how the human brain grows and matures, the primal reflexive brainstem develops first, followed by the emotional centers in the amygdala, and eventually the thinking portion of the brain—the neocortex. This development takes place even into adulthood for college students. The human adult brain uses 20 percent of the body's energy, while an infant's consumes up to 65 percent.[12] Babies are born with virtually all the neurons they will ever need, but what they need most of all is neuronal connections—the place where active learning happens. In other words, infants are born ready to do anything, they just need experiences.

Good teachers create cognitive dissonance by making students cognitively uncomfortable, so they feel motivated to learn, to understand. The classroom needs to be a place of high challenge, but lower stress. High stress impedes the brain's ability to learn. "Listen first to understand and then to be understood" is the mantra of the best classrooms and home environments. Students need to take on a sense of ownership and responsibility for their own learning and begin to worry less about what the teacher wants or what's on the test. They need to develop a sense of self-motivation, a desire to learn, and a practice of reflective metacognition.[13] "[Researchers] have consistently found that most extrinsic motivators [teacher-driven] damage intrinsic motivation."[14]

Again, Materna explained: "Indeed, the avoidance of threat and bodily harm, the search for emotionally satisfying experiences, and the innate need for novelty and stimulation are the driving forces behind learning."[15] These are the attributes of the best teachers and the classroom environments they try to create where students engage in their learning by taking ownership and strive for higher-order thinking, application, and reflection.

Part II then takes us into the realm of learning theory. It explores insights from behavioral, cognitive, and social constructivist approaches to learning. These theories will include the work of noted theorists such as Skinner, Bandura, Piaget, Vygotsky, and Booker T. Washington. Diversity, learner growth and development, and environment all have clear implications for students. In 2018, the National Academies of Sciences, Engineering, and Medicine noted, "Each learner develops a unique array of knowledge and cognitive resources in the course of life that are molded by the interplay of that learner's cultural, social, cognitive, and biological contexts."[16]

Like part I, part II will conclude by describing implications for teaching, classroom environment, the lesson plan, the assignments, and how students' learning is assessed and the effectiveness of classroom instruction. Parts I and II focus on the What—What are the key concepts from brain research and from learning theory? These chapters also begin to develop the So What, or the implications, for today's classrooms.

Part III takes the more general implications described in the first two parts and begins to flesh them out for the reader. More detail and specificity are warranted and will give a roadmap to parents and teachers by helping them determine how best to reach their students. The first half of part III is truly the implications part or more of the So What. More succinctly, this part helps to answer the question, "What are the implications for how we teach our children?"

For example, in his book, *What the Best Professors Do*, Ken Bain focused his research on:

> four fundamental inquiries [which are applicable to any level of student]:
>
> 1. What should my students be able to do intellectually, physically, or emotionally as a result of their learning?
> 2. How can I best help and encourage them to develop those abilities and the habits of the heart and mind to use them?
> 3. How can my students and I best understand the nature, quality, and progress of their learning?
> 4. How can I evaluate my efforts to foster that learning?[17]

Robert Leamnson warned, "During the grandest disquisition, what goes on in the heads of students is not comparable to what goes on in the head of the speaker. That fact has enormous import for the development of good pedagogy."[18] Further, that instructor control of motivation—external motivation, if you will—can negatively impact internal motivation of the learner, and the student will not take ownership for their learning; rather, they will seek the external reward.

The National Research Council commissioned a study to explore "the critical issue of how better to link the findings of research on the science of learning to actual practice in the classroom."[19] In this research, John Bransford and his colleagues warned that teachers have begun to focus on breadth as opposed to depth in their curriculum. It's the notorious paradox of the curriculum that is a mile wide and an inch deep. The worry is instructors spend too much time briefly covering everything and never focusing on anything.

Bransford's group went further in their analysis. Many designs for curriculum, instruction, and assessment practices fail to emphasize the importance of conditionalized or contextualized knowledge. For example, texts often present facts and formulas with little attention to helping students learn the conditions under which they are most useful. Many assessments measure only propositional (factual) knowledge and never ask whether students know when, where, and why to use that knowledge.[20]

Richard Resnick's work was cited by Bransford's committee: "A third contrast between schools and everyday environments is that abstract reasoning is often emphasized in school, whereas contextualized reasoning is often used in everyday settings. Reasoning can be improved when abstract logical arguments are embedded in concrete contexts."[21]

Further, the brain does not commit to memory a precise duplicate of what it experienced or read—there simply is not the available space or energy in the brain to accomplish this. After all, the brain uses about the same amount of energy as a twenty-watt lightbulb. What the brain does, rather than creating a precise memory, is to replicate a generalized version across various regions of the brain. This is an efficient method but is prone to error. Another problem with this process is that incorrect comprehension or original misinformation can remain encoded throughout the brain,[22] referred to as the "continued influence effect."[23] Such memories are quite difficult to change and need purposeful mitigation strategies to correct. In other words, once bad information is learned, it's very difficult to remove it.

The final portion of part III is devoted to application. This part can be viewed as the "hands-on" part or more of the Now What. Using historical contexts and the three main theories of learning as foundational launching pads for how to approach teaching students, case study scenarios are presented with reflection questions to emphasize the nuances of learning and environmental influence. In other words, as an instructor, Now What are the applications to my own classroom and teaching?

How teachers try to reach their students might change. Ken Bain explained: "At the core of most [educators'] ideas about teaching is a focus on what the teacher does rather than on what the students are supposed to learn. . . . In contrast, the best educators thought of teaching as anything they might do to help and encourage students to learn. Teaching is engaging students, engineering an environment in which they learn."[24]

Employers often expect different attributes in their employees than those our schools prepare. According to Bransford and his colleagues, "Society envisions graduates of school systems who can identify and solve problems and can make contributions to society throughout their lifetime—who display the qualities of 'adaptive expertise.' . . . To achieve this vision requires rethinking what is taught, how teachers teach, and how what students learn is assessed."[25]

The actual practice of real authentic learning takes time and practice. The type of learning and teaching takes a great deal of time for both the students and the teachers. In a concluding statement to her book, Jane Healy expressed: "Learning is something that children do, not something that is done to them. You have the wisdom to guide the process but not the power to control it. Listen, watch, have patience, enjoy the journey—and the product will take care of itself."[26]

NOTES

1. Erin Hastings and Robin West, "Goal Orientation and Self-Efficacy in Relation to Memory in Adulthood," *Aging, Neuropsychology, and Cognition* 18, 4 (2011): 471–93.

2. Howard Gardner, *Frames of Mind: The Theory of Multiple Intelligences* (New York: Basic Books, 1983).

3. Daniel Goleman, *Emotional Intelligence* (New York: Bantam, 1997).

4. Robert Sternberg, *Successful Intelligence* (New York: Plume, 1997).

5. Benjamin Bloom, M. Engelhart, E. Furst, Hill, and W. Krathwohl, Taxonomy of Educational Objectives: The Classification of Educational Goals (New York: David McKay Company, 1956).

6. Lorin Anderson and David Krathwohl, eds., *A Taxonomy for Learning, Teaching, and Assessing: A Revision of Bloom's Taxonomy of Educational Objectives* (New York: Longman, 2001). Anderson and Krathwohl (one of the original authors) reframed the original taxonomy from using nouns to describe the levels of objectives to verb or action-oriented descriptors. They also changed the top levels, now considering "create" as a higher-order outcome over "evaluate."

7. Robert Marzano and John Kendall, *The New Taxonomy of Educational Objectives* (Thousand Oaks, CA: Corwin Press, 2006); Grant Wiggins and J. McTighe, *Understanding by Design* (Alexandria, VA: Association for Supervision and Curriculum Development, 2005). Other versions have been created as well, but the work of Anderson and Marzano are the most often cited in educational circles. Debate continues whether the taxonomy truly is a hierarchy or simply a series of different types of learning objectives each independent of one another and of no less or more importance than the others, but simply stating the type. For the sake of this book, the differentiation is more academic and not so relevant. Other derivative versions include affective and psychomotor domains (even Bloom created taxonomies for these domains) and cognitive and mental processes, for example.

8. Eric Jensen and Liesl McConchie, *Brain-Based Learning: Teaching the Way Students Really Learn* (Thousand Oaks, CA: Corwin Press, 2020), 2. Jensen and

McConchie added: "The brain does not learn on demand according to a school's rigid, inflexible schedule" (2).

9. Richard Restak, *The New Brain: How the Modern Age is Rewiring Your Brain* (Emmaus: Pennsylvania: Rodale Press, 2003), 32.

10. Laurie Materna, *Jump Start the Adult Learner: How to Engage and Motivate Adults Using Brain-Compatible Strategies* (Thousand Oaks, CA: Corwin Press, 2007), xii.

11. Robert Sylwester, *A Celebration of Neurons: An Educator's Guide to the Human Brain* (Alexandria, VA: Association for Supervision and Curriculum Development, 1995), 116.

12. Michio Kaku, *The Future of the Mind: The Scientific Quest to Understand, Enhance, and Empower the Mind* (New York: Doubleday, 2014).

13. National Academies of Sciences, Engineering, and Medicine, *How People Learn II: Learners, Contexts, and Cultures* (Washington, DC: The National Academies Press, 2018), 70:

How do people orchestrate their own learning? Three key ways are through metacognition, executive function, and self-regulation. *Metacognition* is the ability to monitor and regulate one's own cognitive processes and to consciously regulate behavior, including affective behavior. . . . *[E]xecutive function*, refers to cognitive and neural processing that involves the overall regulation of thinking and behavior and the higher-order processes that enable people to plan, sequence, initiate, and sustain their behavior toward some goal, incorporating feedback and making adjustments. *Self-regulation* refers to learning that is focused by means of metacognition, strategic action, and motivation to learn. The integration and interrelation of these dimensions of processing is also critical for deeper or higher-order learning, and for the development of complex skills and knowledge such as reasoning, problem solving, and critical thinking.

14. Ken Bain, *What the Best College Teachers Do* (Cambridge, MA: Harvard University Press, 2004), 33.

15. Materna, *Jump Start the Adult Learner*, 25.

16. National Academies, *How People Learn II*, 2.

17. Bain, *What the Best College Teachers Do*, 49.

18. Robert Leamnson, *Thinking about Teaching and Learning: Developing Habits of Learning with First Year College and University Students* (Sterling, VA: Sylus Publishing, 1999), 17.

19. John Bransford, Ann Brown, and Rodney Cocking, eds., *How People Learn: Brain, Mind, Experience, and School* (Washington, DC: National Academy Press, 2000), vii.

20. Bransford, Brown, and Cocking, eds., *How People Learn*, 49.

21. Bransford, Brown, and Cocking, eds., *How People Learn*, 74.

22. K. H. Ecker Ullrich, Briony Swire, and Stephan Lewandowsky, "Correcting Misinformation—A Challenge for Education and Cognitive Science," in *Processing Inaccurate Information: Theoretical and Implied Perspectives from Cognitive Science and the Educational Sciences*, edited by David Rapp and Jason Braasch (Cambridge, MA: The MIT Press, 2014), 15.

23. Colleen Seifert, "The Continued Influence Effect: The Persistence of Misinformation in Memory and Reasoning Following Correction," in *Processing Inaccurate Information: Theoretical and Implied Perspectives from Cognitive Science and the Educational Sciences*, edited by David Rapp and Jason Braasch (Cambridge, MA: The MIT Press, 2014): 39.

24. Bain, *What the Best College Teachers Do*, 48–49.

25. Bransford, Brown, and Cocking, eds., *How People Learn*, 133.

26. Jane Healy, *Your Child's Growing Mind: Brain Development and Learning from Birth to Adolescence* (New York: Broadway Books, 2007), 304.

Part I

The Brain

Remarkable insights into our understanding of the human brain have been made in recent years. This research has led to prescient findings that impact how students learn, how we teach, and how we assess their learning and the effectiveness of our teaching. We have found that the intuitions and practices of the most experienced teachers are supported by these insights with respect to both the science and art of teaching.

Early pronouncements of isolated portions of the brain being solely responsible for learning and memory were spurious. We have come to understand that while various regions of the brain maintain some primacy for different aspects of thinking, learning, and memory, none of this takes place in isolation.[1] The brain doesn't think and learn in isolation from the rest of the body. All this work is part of a complex, dynamic, and even error-prone set of integrated systems. It is from this perspective that we begin our journey into the brain before we move into the more granular aspects of the human mind, specifically how it thinks and learns.

NATURE AND NURTURE

This age-old debate has pitted educators against one other from time immemorial. Is it nature or nurture which impacts student learning the most? Brain researchers and cognitive scientists have settled the debate. It's not either/or; it's both/and. They are emphatic about this point. Both our genetic makeup and our environment play critical interconnected roles in our development. It is nonsensical to talk of one without the other. It comes down to what we do with what we have been given.[2] The implications for parents and teachers are incredible.

Educational psychologist Jane Healy explains: "There is such a constant interaction between basic capacity and experience from the moment of a baby's conception that the question is impossible to answer—and really unnecessary—to answer."[3] Moreover, biology, relationships, social experiences, and culture all play essential roles in brain development.[4]

We do know the human brain is born ready to learn and adapt to do almost anything. It can learn to be fluent in any language and to master untold skills in virtually any field. The neurons and supporting glial cells are there from birth; they just need to make the connections through processes of learning and experiences. A child's brain increases in size by four by the time they reach school age and is 90 percent of the adult brain in volume by that time.[5]

Former professor at the University of Oregon Robert Sylwester wrote *A Celebration of Neurons* for the Association of Supervision and Curriculum Development. This seminal work explains not only brain development but its application to the classroom, as well. He wrote, in part:

> Although most of a brain's lifetime supply of neurons are in place shortly after birth, many of the axon-dendrite connections that process cognitive information develop after birth, as a brain gradually adapts to its environment and makes itself the unique result of its own experience. In the human brain, this post birth development results in a weight increase from about one pound at birth, to two pounds at age one, to three pounds at late adolescent maturation.[6]

The human brain is primed at birth to learn. It actively seeks learning opportunities and challenges. Parents can provide opportunities and encourage use of multiple senses, but at the same time be cautious to not overstimulate the child—they'll let you know when that occurs by turning away, losing focus, or crying out. The parent's role is to provide opportunity, and the child's role is to explore, experiment, and gain experience.[7]

Various portions of the brain grow, develop, and mature at different rates and at different stages. These will be discussed in the pages to come. For now, it is important to understand that our brains continue to physically grow and develop even through college when certain higher cognitive functions fully mature.

Often, we hear how the brain functions and processes information like a computer. Such reasoning is not only faulty, but it leads to poor strategies for teaching. Rather, the human brain grows and functions much more organically and dynamically—a jungle or ecological metaphor, if you will. Neural connections grow while others die off. Connections are intricately woven throughout the brain and across systems. Different portions of the brain work together in a symbiotic process creating memories and new learning.

As such, this natural understanding of the brain explains its predominate and immediate purpose—survival. It is born to survive, to perceive threats, and subsequently to determine the best course of action. If a threat is sensed, the brain goes into survival mode—fight or flight, if you will—and no higher-order functioning or thinking will take place. Thus, implications of intimidating or stress-filled classrooms and exams are profound.

THE UNIFIED WHOLE

To survive, the brain system is intricately interconnected with other body systems. Professors Eric Jensen and Liesl McConchie note: "Most every process runs through multiple systems (sympathetic, digestive, immune, etc.) and engages not one, but multiple structures (prefrontal cortex, hypothalamus, amygdala, etc.) in the brain and body."[8] Robert Sylwester added the endocrine and circulatory systems to this mix: "Our circulatory system transports each blood cell or hormone molecule to any of numerous sites in our body prepared to receive it. It's a simple system that creates a whole body/brain response to a whole body/brain problem."[9] To punctuate the point, Sylwester concluded:

> Our brain, endocrine, and immune systems, long viewed as separate entities, are now seen as an integrated biochemical system. Our emotional system is located principally in our brain, immune, and endocrine systems, but it also affects such organs as our heart, lungs, stomach, and skin.[10]

Not only should we think of the body/brain as a singular unified system, but the brain itself must be considered a singular whole with no part operating by itself.[11] "The brain's functioning is so complex that multiple areas and systems of neural connections must work together for any task. For example, brain scans of adults doing related language activities—listening, reading out loud, reading silently, and thinking up words—show activity scattered all over the brain," according to Dr. Jane Healy.[12]

Awareness, attention, memory, and thinking are distributed throughout the brain. Not any one area is solely responsible for any of these aspects. Again, Healy explains: "Human memory depends upon widespread circuits and chemical interactions as well as specialized areas."[13] Robert Sylwester continued: "Thought emerges out of attention when a continuous, quite active, synchronized firing pattern resonates between a critical mass of related neural networks in the thalamus (which processes the immediate situation) and the cortex (which contains memories related to objects and events in the immediate situation)."[14]

It is believed there are six stages to memory:

1. Sensory: memory from sensory organs which lasts only for an instant
2. Attention: decides which inputs move further into memory

3. Short-term: lasts only a few seconds if not used
4. Working: actively used thoughts and inputs; lasts as long as active
5. Long-term: memory that is stored indefinitely
6. Retrieval: brought back from long-term memory[15]

The hippocampus directs memories to different parts of the brain. Michio Kaku explains that "long-term memories are encoded not electronically, but at the level of protein molecules."[16] Hence, memory reconstruction is a process of encoding and storing experiences in the brain. The encoded memory is not an exact duplicate of the experience. Rather, it is a subjective representation.[17] Memories are malleable as they are stored across various regions of the brain. As other representative memories are stored in these regions, the memories may become commingled, blurred, and edited. As such, educators need to routinely check for students' understanding and misunderstanding.

Eminent psychologist and author of *Finding Flow* Mihalyi Csikszentmihalyi writes, "Emotions, intentions, and thoughts do not pass through consciousness as separate strands of experience, but that they are constantly interconnected, and modify each other as they go along."[18] Describing, for example, the complexity of learning and playing music, Daniel Levitin notes:

At a neural level, playing an instrument requires the orchestration of regions in our primitive, reptilian brain—the cerebellum and the brain stem—as well as higher cognitive systems such as the motor cortex (in the parietal lobe) and the planning regions of our frontal lobes, the most advanced region of the brain.[19]

Perhaps the most comprehensive description of the regions of the human brain, the various parts, and their unique primacy with respect to education, as well as the intricacies of their interactions with one another, is provided by former nursing professor Laurie Materna. She describes the three primary regions of the brain including the lower, middle, and upper regions.[20] The first is the more primitive brain stem which sits atop the spinal column. This leads to the surrounding middle brain and then ultimately to the upper and outer brain. (Refer to the notes and later in this part for greater detail.)

The lower brain is the first to develop—out of necessity—for this is the region responsible for our survival. It is the middle and upper regions that take longer to mature and much longer to develop intellectually. Some of the higher-functioning areas won't develop until adolescence and even young adulthood. The frontal lobes, the executive control center of the brain, may not fully mature for thirty years!

If the brain—the lower brain—senses the person may be in danger, the whole body goes into survival mode and higher-order thinking will not occur. If the student feels they will be embarrassed or humiliated, they will focus their attention on "saving face," or getting out of the classroom or awkward situation, certainly not on the learning objective for the day. Should the student feel their emotional or mental survival is not an issue, the middle brain or the limbic system becomes activated.

These portions of the brain devoted to producing emotions help long-term memories take root. It is in these two lower regions of the brain that the individual determines the relevancy of what is to be learned. If the concept is found to be relevant, it will likely be moved to short-term working memory and perhaps then on to long-term memory if the concept is actively engaged. Then the neocortex of the upper and outer layer of the brain, responsible for higher-level thinking, is activated. In this way, the whole brain continues to work together with stored long-term memories in both the emotional portions of the brain and with the thinking regions of the brain.

Emotions are critical according to both brain research and to learning theory. If the learning environment is positive, on the one hand, the brain will more likely focus on the teaching objective and instigate higher-level thinking. If, on the other hand, the learning environment is negative, the brain will downshift into a more survival mode and limit thinking. As such, emotion is the trigger point to what comes next. Relevance and an emotionally supportive environment lay the foundation for learning.

As has been discussed, learning and thinking are not isolated endeavors to particular parts of the brain. The entire brain is involved in all cognition even though certain areas may have primacy over others for certain aspects. We're fortunate this is the case, for in instances of traumatic injury to a certain region of the brain, other regions can still carry on because of their memories and associated abilities. This inherent redundancy in brain functioning and the brain's plasticity are crucial to our survival.

Cognition and memories are strengthened, as a matter of fact, by rich experiences and by activating multiple regions of the brain using the different senses. The more senses involved and the more experiences we have, the greater the ability to remember and to think at higher levels. Most learners (40 to 65 percent) would be considered visual learners, according to Colin Rose. Auditory learners comprise another 25 to 30 percent, and 5 to 15 percent are primarily kinesthetic learners.[21] Think of the implications for your classroom.

Figure 1.1 shows various parts of the cortex and their primacy in various learning modalities.

Now let us turn our attention to a more granular description of the various regions and subregions of the human brain—to learn their primary roles and how they interact with one another. Then we can focus on how our children's brains grow and develop before we move to implications for our own teaching and assessment strategies.

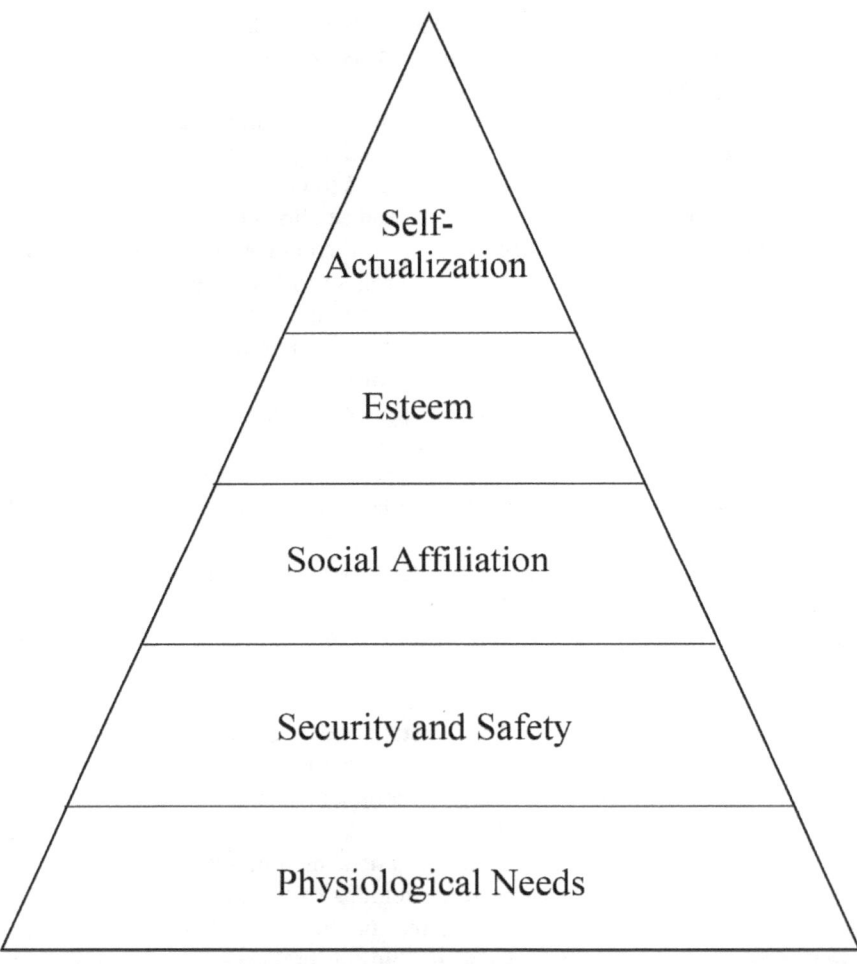

Figure 1.1 Brain Regions Where Learning Takes Place *Source:* **Created by Dr. Toni Bailey**

NEURONS

The most fundamental units of our brain are the cells. The brain is made up of two primary types of cells: the neurons and the glial cells. We consider the neurons as the thinking cells associated with the brain, while the glial cells are the support cells to the neurons.

Glial cells far outnumber the neurons which they support. Our brains have trillions of glial cells which provide nutrition to the neurons, help to repair the neurons, and protect the neurons from harmful bacteria. Glial cells also produce the protein myelin which coats and protects neurons as they become more active. The myelin coating, or sheath, further helps the neurons to fire quicker and more efficiently. It has been reported that Albert Einstein's brain had a larger number of glial cells compared to the average person.[22]

A child is born with virtually all the neurons they will ever need, estimated between one hundred billion or even up to one trillion. That is nature; the rest is the nurture. A child's brain is born with the ability to learn any language fluently, to learn any musical instrument, to acquire thinking skills for any task that they are given. The neurons are there from the beginning.

What the newborn brain cells do not have are the enormous array of interconnections with other neurons and other regions of the brain which an adult brain acquires through experience—through learning. The brain can adjust and learn because of its immense capability to adapt and to make new connections—a term called "plasticity"—a process that can last a lifetime.

The neuron is an amazing cell. (See figure 1.2 for detail about neurons and how they connect.) We are born with virtually all the neurons we will ever need. The more a neuron is stimulated through use—experience or learning, if you will—the stronger it becomes. It doesn't become stronger by itself in isolation, however; it becomes stronger with its interconnections with other neurons and nerves. The process of connecting to other neurons is called neural branching. Neurons can connect to thousands of other neurons. Cells that are not used or activated through stimulation become weaker and eventually wither away—a process called neural pruning.

"Neural networks are collections of neurons that constantly rewire and reinforce themselves after learning a new task," according to Michio Kaku in *The Future of the Mind*.[23] He goes on to add, "Neural networks are parallel, with one hundred billion neurons firing at the same time in order to accomplish one goal: to learn."

Indeed, the difference between an infant's brain and adult's brain is not the number of neurons so much as the number of connections or synapses. As such, the infant's brain weighs approximately one pound and doubles in weight during the first year. By the time the child reaches young adulthood, their brain has reached three pounds. Even the very act of thinking causes the neurons to fire and to strengthen just as it does with physical sensing or activity.

As can be seen from figure 1.2, each neuron has a cell body with dendrite spines on one end. These dendrites receive chemical signals, or neurotransmitters,[24] from other cells. The cell body turns the chemical signal into an electrical impulse which travels down the cell's axon (up to a meter in length or more) where it gets turned back into a chemical at the synaptic junction between the neuron and thousands of other neurons in its region. No neuron directly touches another; rather, they are awash in a chemical bath with other neurons—sending and receiving, stimulating or inhibiting, further action. The process of thinking causes cells to communicate, as described by Professor Laurie Materna:

> Each time the brain thinks a thought, these connections are fired up, modifying the electrochemical wiring. The more novel and stimulating the thought is, the more likely it will activate a new connection . . . [which] trigger the electrochemical process that promotes long-term memory.[25]

Thinking and memories are created when groups or networks of neurons fire across regions of the brain. No area is solely responsible for a particular thought or memory. Each network is responsible for a portion of the thinking or memory, but together they complete the whole picture. Likewise, people's memories are not exact copies of an event. Rather, they are an approximate reconstruction and are thus prone to error when recalled.[26]

Sylwester added, "Thought emerges out of attention when a continuous, quite active, synchronized firing pattern resonates between a critical mass of related neural networks in the thalamus (which processes the immediate situation) and the cortex (which contains memories)."[27] Each associated neuron is part of the entire thought or memory. The more often these neurons fire with additional thinking or experiences, the stronger they become and the easier it becomes for them to be re-activated—they become more efficient.

Thus, in the words of Dr. Richard Restak, "Intelligence is plastic and modifiable. All of our experiences result in the formation of neuronal circuits. The richer, more varied, and more challenging the experiences, the more elaborate the neuronal circuits."[28] This learning is caused by the brain systematically weaving together past experiences within the current context.

How are such tiny neurons able to interact in such complex ways across various regions of the brain instantaneously? Recent scientific breakthroughs provide answers. Cognitive scientist and philosophy professor at the University of British Columbia Evan Thompson explains in part that the brain produces electromagnetic fields (or neuroelectric fields):

> When many neurons are interconnected to formal neural networks, the sum or superposition of their electrical fields generates macroscopic neuroelectrical fields at a higher level of complexity. . . . Collectively, however, neurons synchronize their action potentials, both locally and across large distances, and this temporal synchronization of an enormous number of action potentials produces the coherent and large-scale electrodynamical states of the brain that correlate with various modes of consciousness.[29]

Further, some researchers have concluded that neural synapses communicate in quantum wave patterns, enabling communication to occur throughout the brain in an instant in incalculable ways. Michael Talbot went as far as to consider the human brain a model of holographic thinking. Citing the work of Austrian neuroscientist Karl Pribram, Talbot recognized each neuron held a partial piece of a thought's or a memory's full picture, but through complex interference patterns in the synapses, a full holographic image emerges.[30]

Neurons and glial cells are the most fundamental units found throughout every region of the brain. It is now time to discuss the various regions from the most primitive portion (the brain stem) to the most advanced region (the cortex)—the part that makes us uniquely human and capable of intricate, creative, and elaborate thinking.

BRAIN GROWTH AND DEVELOPMENT

The human brain, like that of animals, is primed foremost for survival. Humans, however, have advanced brains which are capable of great learning, creativity, and cognition. Such great abilities take time to develop after survival is ensured. Robert Sylwester explained it this way:

> The basic genetic developmental pattern for our brain is thus quite simple and straightforward: (1) create an initial excess of cells and connections among related areas—in effect, temporarily wire up everything to everything, (2) use emotion, experience, and learning to strengthen the useful connections, and then prune away the unused and inefficient, and (3) maintain enough synaptic flexibility (commonly called *plasticity*) to allow neural network connections to shift about throughout life as conditions change and new problem-solving challenges emerge.[31]

As has been noted earlier, one way to think of the brain is with it encapsulating three main sections—a triune brain—the lower brain (the survival brain), the middle brain (the brain associated with emotion and working memory), and the upper brain (the brain regions devoted to rational, creative, long-term memory, and higher-order thinking). These areas will be described in greater detail later in this part.

Different regions of the brain, just like the rest of the human body, mature and develop at different rates and at different critical times. Often, parents worry that their child is not making cognitive gains at the same time or pace their peers might be. Most likely the child is making physical gains in other parts of their body, motor development, for example, instead. Or portions of their brain are developing which cannot be as easily observed. In either case, a child's brain and body are always developing on their own timetable,[32] and it is best not to rush it, but be prepared when it is ready. In other words, it is unnecessary and perhaps counterproductive to worry and to force learning when the child's brain is not developmentally ready. Healy noted:

> *Your overall goal should be not to "teach" your baby, but to help her discover how to organize experience for herself* [italics in original]. Most babies give explicit clues about what kind of input is needed and let you know when it's overpowering or not interesting anymore. Explaining things to children won't do the job; they must have the chance to experience, wonder, experiment, and act it out for themselves.[33]

Because it is devoted to our survival, the lower brain is virtually primed at birth to function immediately and to respond to the environment. It takes in sensory inputs to determine whether a flight or fight response is warranted, or if further processing by the middle brain is appropriate. As such, the middle brain takes longer to mature, and even its different regions develop at different rates.

The most advanced portions of the brain, those in the upper region, take the longest to mature and develop, often times into adulthood, and are ever adapting or learning.[34] Educational psychology professors Jeanne Ellis Ormrod and Brett Jones stipulated, "The prefrontal cortex—the part of the brain responsible for planning, decision making, and many other advanced reasoning processes—is especially slow to mature and doesn't take on a truly adultlike form until individuals reach their early 20s."[35]

It's the prefrontal cortex (or the executive center of the brain) which is associated with reasoning, long-term memory, self-control, attention, planning, and judgment, and is the last area of the brain to mature.[36] The frontal lobes prune neurons that an individual's experience shows to be irrelevant or unnecessary. This is also the critical time when myelination is making its greatest impact on the cortex. The implications of this knowledge have great importance for parents and teachers alike, as we will see later in subsequent pages.

The process of learning makes physical and structural changes to the brain. Learning creates more synapses, strengthens the neurons and connections that already exist making them more efficient, and the cortex gains weight the more it is used. And not only does the brain modify itself through its plasticity, but it builds in redundancy and distributes learning across various regions of the brain. "To continue to function after a brain injury requires that a blow to a single part of the brain doesn't shut down the whole system. Important brain systems evolved additional, supplementary pathways," according to neuroscientist Daniel Levitin.[37]

All of learning is interconnected throughout the brain. We know memories and thinking don't reside in only particular regions of the brain, but these various parts impact the complete learning experience. Further, these brain regions affect various systems throughout the entire body. For example, according to Sylwester,

> The principal brain mechanisms involved in procedural memories are the amygdala (our brain's emotional center located in the limbic system), the cerebellum (located in the lower back of the brain), and the autonomic nervous system (which regulates circulation and respiration)—but procedural memories also involve altered muscle systems.[38]

So, even the very act of thinking impacts the brain itself—it strengthens neurons, creates additional synapses, and furthers interconnectivity throughout the brain, indeed, throughout the body. Even dreams activate the same neurons and regions of the brain as do waking experiences and thinking.[39]

REGIONS OF THE BRAIN

As previously noted, there are three primary levels of the human brain: lower, middle, and upper. Each has increasing complexity, takes longer to develop and mature, and plays escalating roles in our intelligence. We'll start with a brief overview of the most basic and primitive portion of the human brain—the lower brain.[40]

The lower brain consists of the brain stem and the cerebellum. The brain stem sits atop the spinal cord and is the terminus of all the senses, except for smell. It regulates our body's functions of respiration and blood circulation. It is the brain stem which has primary responsibility to sense danger. If it does sense danger, it automatically sets us on the path to fight, flight, freeze, or fawn. As such, further advanced cognition does not take place, unless the person purposefully and rationally considers the circumstances to determine whether other options are better. A student who feels threatened in the classroom likely will focus more on survival—saving face—than on the lesson's objective for the day—it's only natural they do so.

The cerebellum is the other portion of the lower brain and is responsible for physical movement and kinesthetic memories. This region of the brain has more neurons than the rest of the brain regions combined, and it connects with all regions at the same time. Thus, it plays a central role in coordinating thoughts and memories and processing information, including our most high-level cognition. Further, the cerebellum helps us operate at a subconscious level—on autopilot—if you will. Such activities as walking and dreaming, for example, operate here.

Materna explained: "Procedural memories (muscle memory) are accessed through the cerebellum . . . and are best recalled unconsciously."[41] Procedural memories are not limited to this region of the brain, as noted earlier, however. The cerebellum is interconnected with all areas of the brain. In this way, the cerebellum works in tandem with the brain stem's circulation and respiratory systems, and the limbic system (the emotional region of the middle brain) for procedural memories. Because of its integral role in thinking and its central role in physical behavior, implications for teaching are profound and will be discussed in greater detail later in this part and again in part III.

The middle brain is more advanced and takes longer to develop than the lower brain. It is known as the limbic system, encases the brain stem and cerebellum, and contains the thalamus (senses), hippocampus (memories), and amygdala (emotions). The middle brain is responsible for our hormonal and immune systems and for regulating emotions. As such, it connects with our prefrontal cortex as a system check to determine the best response to a given emotional scenario and ties memories to emotions. The limbic system urges action, while the prefrontal cortex urges restraint. While the limbic system sits atop the brain stem and cerebellum, it is surrounded by the neocortex. It is the neocortex which operates at the conscious level; the limbic system works at the unconscious level.

For educators, the limbic system plays a critical role for intrapersonal intelligence. Robert Sylwester explained that this doesn't occur fully until adulthood or late adolescence when the frontal lobes and the prefrontal cortex have matured. Physically, the brain naturally has an emotional response to an input *before* the rational portions of the brain have a chance to respond. As such, it takes conscientious effort to control one's emotions by allowing the executive center of the brain to take the lead.[42]

The thalamus is the processing point for all our senses except smell. "It helps to initiate consciousness and make preliminary classifications of external information," according to Fred Alan Wolf.[43] This organ then further processes incoming information on to the thinking portions of our brain—the cortex—for a more detailed analysis, and it serves as the holding area for short-term memory and attention. It also sends information to the amygdala to determine whether a self-defense posture is necessitated. In this sense, it communicates with the rest of the brain about the outside world. The related hypothalamus regulates important molecules in between our endocrine and nervous systems.

"The hippocampus is responsible for making meaning out of stored memories and converting information from working memory to long-term memory," according to Materna.[44] Like the thalamus, the hippocampus also works directly with the brain's cortex and is important for the learning of facts and rules.[45] In an interesting aside, the wishbone-shaped hippocampus (one located in each hemisphere) is one of the few areas of the brain that can generate new neurons, or the process known as neurogenesis. According to Ormrod and Jones, "The hippocampus also seems to be a central figure in learning, in that it pulls together information it simultaneously receives from various parts of the brain."[46]

The amygdala—again, one in each hemisphere—plays a key role in processing emotions, especially negative emotions such as fear. According to Jensen and McConchie, "The amygdala's primary task is to ensure our survival."[47] It also works directly with the brain's higher-level cortex. It is responsible for long-term memories associated with emotions. In so doing, when a long-term memory is accessed, the amygdala brings along the emotion associated with that memory. It sends its signals on to the hippocampus.

When any of these middle brain regions (thalamus, hippocampus, amygdala) are activated, they send out a combination of neurotransmitters and hormones. This, in part, is one of the reasons emotions play such a critical role in learning and memories. As always, the implications for teachers and parents are incredible and should not be underappreciated. Using emotions positively can help retrieve and strengthen memories and recall as well as automatically activate advanced regions of the brain. It is important to note that too much stress, especially negative stress, can cause the hippocampus to shrink. The best educators try to create a classroom environment and curriculum of high challenge but low stress.

The upper brain is what most people think about when we consider education. This region, the cerebrum, contains 85 percent of the brain's mass and takes the longest to develop and mature (into our twenties) and is often what we refer to as gray matter. It contains the two complementary hemispheres, connected by the corpus callosum, and is divided into four lobes: frontal, temporal, parietal, and occipital. The cerebrum is wrapped by a thin layer—six layers of neurons—known as the neocortex which we consider the thinking part of the brain. According to Ormrod and Jones:

Complex thinking, learning, and knowledge are located primarily in the upper and outer parts of the brain collectively known as the cortex. . . . The portion of the cortex located near the forehead, known as the prefrontal cortex, is largely responsible for a wide variety of distinctly human activities, including sustained attention, reasoning, planning, decision making, coordinating complex activities, and preventing nonproductive thoughts and behaviors.[48]

It is in this portion of the brain where complex thinking takes place. Here we find the processes of problem-solving, creativity, analysis, synthesis, and evaluation—the higher levels on Bloom's Taxonomy.[49] While the limbic system is often referred to as the brain's inner shell, the cortex can be referred to as its outer shell. Further, while the limbic system is better known for concerning itself with negative emotions and fight or flight responses, the prefrontal cortex regulates such emotions as empathy, compassion, and altruism.[50] Interestingly, Andrew Holecek explains:

> The prefrontal cortex is deactivated when we sleep. This part of the brain is involved with "executive function," which relates to the ability to determine good and bad, to differentiate between conflicting thoughts, to predict outcomes, to apply moral values, and to moderate social behavior... the prefrontal cortex isn't fully developed until age twenty-five, which leads to bad decisions and poor social control. Executive function is "parental" function.[51]

Neurons in the cortex are bundled together into narrow strands, each of which is responsible for specific functions or sensory information. They interconnect with one another, both vertically and horizontally, and come together to paint a clear picture or interpretation of the information being processed.[52] For example, one bundle may be responsible for interpreting a particular sound, while others are responsible for other individual sounds. When intertwined together, they understand a complete piece of music. Couple this neural collection with other neural columns interpreting various visual and other sensory inputs, previous knowledge, memories, and emotions, a staggering and dynamic interplay of neural network activity comes together for a complete experience.

The cerebrum, as noted, is divided into four lobes in each hemisphere. The frontal lobes are located behind the forehead. They consist of the motor cortex and the prefrontal cortex. The former coordinates our physical activity. The prefrontal cortex is responsible for higher-level thinking, planning, and abstract reasoning, in particular. It controls our conscious behavior and integrates working memory. Importantly, our frontal lobes help to regulate our emotions and judgments and can keep us from overreacting to emotionally charged situations. This is the executive control center of our brain; it's the region which matures last and is the region we need to teach students how to use to make wise decisions.

The temporal lobes are located above each ear and are responsible for hearing, memory, and meaning making. These lobes also play a role in language. The parietal lobes, which are located across the top of the cerebrum, are responsible for sensory processing such as touch and spatial understanding. They also play a primary role in language processing. Across the back of the head are the occipital lobes, which process visual information.

While each regional lobe has primary areas of responsibility associated with it, when each is activated, the other regions are activated as well in a highly orchestrated fashion—they do not work in isolation from one another. Together, they recognize and create patterns and meaning and knowledge.

They retrieve experiences from memory and create new memories. Up to 99 percent of this activity is unconscious. According to Materna: "Implications for education are profound: Learners are unconsciously absorbing, interpreting, and acting upon environmental cues over and above the actual lesson presented to their conscious minds."[53]

On a related topic, Douglas Hacker expressed that under normal conditions people overlook errors 40 percent of the time in their text reading.[54] Most likely they lose focus or are rushed for time. They may overlook misinformation in the writing or not fully comprehend what they have simply scanned. Again, the implications are breathtaking. Student reading needs to be purposeful, focused, and deliberate. Approaches need to be used to check student understanding before incorrect learning is transferred into long-term memory which then becomes increasingly difficult to correct.

Once correct or incorrect information is processed or encoded in the brain, it is there. It cannot be simply erased like a computer model. Even more, the information or memory is not simply located in one place—it's diffused across the brain. So, learning is robust, but so is incorrect learning. It is difficult to relearn something correctly once learned incorrectly. It takes deliberative effort and time to compensate or correct.

A great deal has been made about the brain's two hemispheres and how we identify ourselves as either right-brained or left-brained. Much of this discussion has been overblown, yet differences between the cerebral hemispheres do exist. The two distinct halves, or lobes, are connected by a thick band of millions of fibrous neural cells known as the corpus callosum. The corpus callosum is the pathway for communication and collaboration between the two hemispheres. It's critical for the two hemispheres to have their efforts coordinated through the corpus callosum. In the words of Robert Sylwester:

The left hemisphere (in most people) processes the objective content of language—*what* was said—while the right hemisphere processes the emotional content of facial expressions, gestures, and language intonation—*how* it was said. By processing related information from different perspectives, the hemispheres collaborate to produce something that becomes a unified mental experience.[55]

Lateralization among the two hemispheres does exist. Language, speech, and logical thinking primarily take place in the left hemisphere, while the right hemisphere plays a more dominate role in visual and spatial tasks.[56] The lobe sizes differ in the two hemispheres. For example, the right frontal lobe is larger than its counterpart, while the left occipital lobe is larger than the right. In addition, the left hemisphere contains more dopamine, while the right half contains more norepinephrine.[57]

Michio Kaku explains, "The left brain is the dominant one and makes the final decisions. Commands pass from the left brain to the right brain via the corpus callosum."[58] The right hemisphere generally sees or synthesizes the whole picture and is intuitive, empathetic, and artistic, while the left is sequential, analytical, mathematical, and detail oriented. The bottom line, however, is that both hemispheres work together for full understanding—the strengths of both hemispheres must work together for optimal learning to take place. The right hemisphere matures earlier than the left hemisphere.[59]

In a very interesting insight, Andrew Holecek notes that lucid dreams activate the brain in the same way as waking life. If you work on a math problem in your dream, for example, your left hemisphere is stimulated just as it would be during the day. If you sing in your dream, the right hemisphere is activated.[60] Leonard Shlain also notes an intriguing insight: "Each hemisphere of the brain controls the muscles of the body's opposite side. . . . To ensure versatility in case of injury, each hemisphere has some capacity to perform the other side's functions."[61]

The left hemisphere may be more responsible for routine information processing and the right more for novel situations. The left hemisphere is considered more rational, analytical, and logical, while the right hemisphere is more intuitive, integrative, and relational. The left analyzes the details, and the right sees the big picture. If a student reads a passage in the text, their left hemisphere takes primacy. If they encounter a photograph as they read, their right hemisphere may take the lead.[62]

Likewise, when students process language, "the right hemisphere helps with the conceptual understanding, whereas the left is adept with the sequence and the grammar," according to Jane Healy.[63] Both hemispheres work together for a comprehensive understanding. Thus, discussions of right- or left-brained learners are too simplistic. See figure 1.3 for clarity.

Before we turn our attention to general implications for educators and parents, it will be worth a visit to the literature with respect to what we know about how the brains of experts and geniuses work. It has been determined that, organically speaking, experts in some fields have more neurons and neuron connections than nonexperts.[64]

According to John Bransford and his colleagues, experts—because of their extensive knowledge and experience—organize and analyze information differently than most people. These authors note key differences and implications for teaching:

1. "Experts notice features and meaningful patterns of information that are not noticed by novices.
2. Experts have acquired a great deal of content knowledge that is organized in ways that reflect a deep understanding of their subject matter.

3. Experts' knowledge cannot be reduced to sets of isolated facts or propositions but, instead, reflects contexts of applicability: that is, the knowledge is "conditionalized" on a set of circumstances.
4. Experts can flexibly retrieve important aspects of their knowledge with little attentional effort.
5. Though experts know their disciplines thoroughly, this does not guarantee that they are able to teach others.
6. Experts have varying levels of flexibility in their approach to new situations."[65]

In terms of giftedness, Jane Healy created her own list of attributes of these students. They:

1. Take more time to think strategically about problems and less time to solve them.
2. Seek wholes, patterns, and relationships.
3. "Web" knowledge (that is, establish mental categories and connect new ideas to them).
4. Prefer complexity.
5. View learning as an adventure.
6. Possess significant self-discipline to plan and implement projects.[66]

In looking at the brains of musicians, Robert Sylwester explains:

For most people, music processing is centered in the right hemisphere (though rhythm is one element of music processed in the left hemisphere). . . . Trained musicians often activate left hemisphere mechanisms while listening to music, probably because they are also analyzing the music.[67]

Daniel Levitin explains in greater detail why this may be the case. "Musical training appears to have the effect of shifting some music processing from the right (imagistic) hemisphere to the left (logical) hemisphere, as musicians learn to talk about—and perhaps think about—music using linguistic terms."[68]

Such research gives educators hope that they can help develop latent talent in students, while perhaps not to the level of genius, certainly to the level of competence or even expertise. "Following certain brain-based guidelines anyone can achieve expert performance in sports, athletics, and academic pursuits," according to Richard Restak.[69] Restak added to the view that musicians modify their brain organization through focus and repetition—moving the focus from the right to the left hemisphere. Specifically referring to genius, he notes they have a particular internal drive and focus:

> [Geniuses] exhibited an intense concentration, leading to heightened awareness of each of the many components of their actions coupled with an ability to adapt in ways that led to higher levels of control. . . . [They have] "a rage to master": the willingness of the genius, prodigy, or superior performer to devote almost all waking hours to mastering his or her chosen field of endeavor.[70]

In his study of chess grand masters, Restak discovered that they are better at accessing long-term memories as they have an extensive repertoire of experiences. This vast experience, coupled with an earnest focus, gives them the ability to "recognize positions and problems and to retrieve the solutions."[71] These grand masters "don't have to think; they are recognizing patterns"[72] which can be retrieved effortlessly. To which he adds:

> The expert . . . golfer, by mentally attending to extremely subtle aspects of his performance during practice sessions, has successfully transferred this knowledge into working memory within his frontal lobes. Later, when under pressure, his brain concentrates on one or more components of his learned procedural skills. For him, task and not ego remain at the forefront of mental activity.[73]

What we have discovered from how the brain learns, recalls memories, creates, makes decisions, and understands has significant implications for the school classroom. The implications should not only impact the way we teach, but the types of assignments we give and how we assess how well the students have learned and how effectively we have taught them.

GENETIC INFLUENCES

The field of neuro-epigenetics is concerned with the idea of determining to what degree environmental and inherited genes are responsible for various cognitive abilities and functions. There are 20,300 genes in the human genome, and researchers have determined that of these there are nearly nine hundred genes that contribute to cognition.[74]

How our cognitive genes express themselves depends on both nature and nurture. That is, our genes express themselves in a variety of alleles, because of both inherited DNA and responses to the environment, according to Bueno.[75] Heritability is the term used by geneticists to describe how much of a trait is determined by our genes and how much is determined by environmental influences. For example, if a particular trait is 30 percent dependent upon genetics, it is 70 percent dependent upon the environment.

Research indicates that our environments can influence how our genes express themselves.[76] Our bodies can make "epigenetic modifications" to respond to what is happening in our environment.[77] Traits such as high intelligence, cooperativity, grit, and attention focus have heritability percentages of 33 percent, 13 percent, 37 percent, and 28 percent, respectively.[78] This concept is significant to educators because it implies that teachers' pedagogical approaches, in many cases, create environmental influences that may cause students' genes to express themselves in either proactive or inactive ways.

IMPLICATIONS

The implications for the classroom are profound and should lead to significant changes in our learning environments. Many teaching practices of the best educators have been affirmed, and other new challenges have now become evident. While the first half of part III provides greater detail of educational implications and the final half of part III shares concrete examples of curriculum, assignments, and assessments based on these implications, a general overview highlighting these general implications is warranted here.

To meet the needs of our society and the demands for today's workforce, educators from our PK–12 school systems must take a careful re-examination of their curriculum, their pedagogy, their strategies for assessment, their entire classroom experience, and how they relate to their broader communities.

With the student's brain in mind, parents and teachers must understand how the brain learns, accesses memories, creates knowledge, and solves problems. Robert Sylwester explains, "[b]ecause neurons thrive only in an environment that stimulates them to receive, store, and transmit information, the challenge to educators is simple: define, create, and maintain an emotionally and intellectually stimulating school environment and curriculum."[79] As most of their learning happens at the subconscious level, the classroom environment is crucial.

It is difficult to separate the implications for curriculum, pedagogy, assessment, and the classroom environment from one another as they are all so intricately interrelated. Discussion of teaching incorporates factions of each of these areas as they meld into one another—much like how the brain itself is organized and learns. What follows, however, is an attempt to differentiate key implications in each of these areas beginning with key points about the learner's brain.

The Brain

We know that throughout a person's life their brain's synapses continue to grow—to make complex connections. This plasticity enables new learning to occur throughout one's lifespan and to overcome previous obstacles. "Lasting brain change occurs when new inputs are perceived as highly relevant or compelling," according to Eric Jensen.[80]

The brain is designed first and foremost for survival—to protect the person. If the brain—the lower brain—senses the person may be in danger, the whole body goes into survival mode and higher-level thinking will not occur. If the student feels they will be embarrassed or humiliated, they will focus their attention on "saving face," or getting out of the classroom, certainly not on the objective for the day. If, though, the student should feel their survival is not an issue, the middle brain—the limbic system—becomes activated.

It is here where the brain seeks relevance and becomes emotionally involved with the context and integrates with memory. Even here, though, the brain can prevent the student from higher-order thinking. "When the amygdala senses uncertainty in any form—physical, emotional, or even social—it harnesses all the brain's energy to focus on the potential threat. This means any cognitive functioning will be at best impaired, if not temporarily halted. . . . [Some students] get lost in the emotional processing and lose focus on learning," according to Jensen.[81]

The sage educator will ensure an emotionally safe classroom environment and harness the power of emotions. This will allow necessary time for other regions of the brain to become actively involved and to integrate working memory with long-term memory. It is the middle and upper regions of the brain that take longer to mature and much longer to develop. Some of the higher-functioning areas won't develop until adolescence and even young adulthood. These are the students in your classrooms—those whose higher-level thinking is still maturing.

The frontal lobes, the executive portion of the brain, may not fully mature for thirty years! Parents and teachers should help guide the student's growth and use of the executive center—to help them slow down, be thoughtful in their analysis, and to be purposeful in their decision-making and their responses.[82] Adults need to model and reinforce metacognitive and deliberative problem-solving practices.

The entire brain needs to be engaged, preferably through multiple senses, for optimal student learning. Students need to feel safe and able to take intellectual risks. Their emotions will drive attention as they search for relevance and connections to previous learning and experiences. They will automatically engage both hemispheres, and the more we can do to support such efforts, the better their learning will be.[83] We need to help them take the time and effort to utilize the executive center of their brains which will better engage their higher-order thinking capabilities.

The human brain is a social brain and learns best when working with others. It needs time to think, to reflect, and to integrate what it is learning or experiencing. It needs mental breaks. Multiple avenues of teaching and learning need to be incorporated as some students are primarily visual learners (40 to 65 percent) and others auditory (25 to 30 percent) or kinesthetic (5 to 15 percent). The brain seeks to make connections to previous memories and experiences. It wants relevancy and novelty, and the brain is always looking for patterns and relationships to understand the big picture. As such, the brain can adapt.

In other words, we need to give students the opportunities to stretch those advanced areas of their brains, to think about their own thinking strategies—metacognition—and we need to model these behaviors for them. In turn, this understanding of how the brain works will impact our curriculum, our pedagogy, our classroom environment, and how we assess our students, as well as the effectiveness of our own teaching.

The Classroom and Its Environment

The classroom needs to provide an environment that supports what we know best about how the brain learns. If a student should feel threatened by an intimidating teaching style or being embarrassed in front of their classmates, they will be stuck in a primitive low-level cognitive mode. We expect higher-order thinking, so we need to create an atmosphere that supports it.

This means we need to focus on the learner and their learning. We need to move from teacher-oriented classrooms and instruction to one that supports learning. K–12 teachers have for quite some time helped to create a learner-centered classroom where students take on more ownership of their own learning. Some teachers have even now moved beyond the phrase "*learner*-centered" to the notion of "*learning*-centered" classrooms.

In either case, educators will want to ensure their classrooms aren't intimidating places that create high levels of stress. Students need to be able to feel comfortable enough to struggle with ideas and to explore their own thinking and the topics at hand without the worry of reprisal from the teacher or fellow classmates. Students need to be free to make mistakes and learn from them. While some stress may be beneficial—in the form of challenge—we must not create an atmosphere whereby students just want to escape. We need to think in terms of high challenge but low stress. Eric Jensen stipulated that up to 90 percent of the input our brains receive enters at the unconscious level.[84] The classroom environment is critical.

We know that the human brain is a social brain. People often learn best through their interactions with others, or social learning. The key takeaway here, however, is the need for students to have opportunities to work with one another at some point during the lesson. Students learn different approaches to understanding from their peers, and they learn better by sharing their own approaches, as well. Likewise, the teacher needs to be responsive to the needs of all learners.

Zaretta Hammond[85] provides an informative framework for teaching students with cultural responsiveness to engage the brain. Her research emphasizes that the brain must feel safe and culturally considered because to a certain degree, our brains are uploaded with cultural "software" due to the cultural norms that we have been exposed to throughout our lives.

These cultural norms that we were exposed to since birth essentially contribute to our realities and dispositions toward the world. Therefore, the "hardware" of our brains will respond to environmental stimuli because of how the stimuli align with our cultural understandings of the world. Thus, the cultural responsiveness or lack thereof in a classroom environment can influence the fight, flight, freeze, and fawn response.

John Bransford and his colleagues have put together a short list of practices they recommend be instituted for today's classrooms. It provides an erudite summation of the implications covered over the previous pages. This list is paraphrased with interpretation as follows:

1. Schools and classrooms must be learner-centered with the focus on each student and their learning. This requires an approach of differentiation in teaching practices. Faculty need to present students with "just manageable difficulties." This means tasks need to be challenging enough to maintain engagement but not so difficult as to lead to discouragement.
2. Attention must be given to what is taught (information, subject matter), why it is taught (understanding), and what competence or mastery looks like. Learning with understanding is often harder to accomplish than simply memorizing, and it takes more time. We must disabuse ourselves of a curriculum that is a mile wide and an inch deep. Focus must be given to essential concepts with in-depth study and understanding. Likewise, our tests often reinforce memorizing rather than understanding. So, we will need to look to better align our testing approaches with higher-level thinking.
3. Formative assessment needs to play an ever-increasing role in our classrooms. Real-time formative assessments are those quick and informal checks designed to determine student understanding as lessons progress. Such assessments help both the professor and the student determine if they're on the right track or whether more instruction is needed.

Quizzes for the sake of grading are not as relevant. "Gotcha quizzes" are less appropriate and unnecessary where students have ownership in their own learning. In sum, formative assessments provide students with opportunities to revise and improve their thinking, help students see their own progress, and help teachers identify problems that need to be remedied.

1. Learning is influenced in fundamental ways by the context in with it takes place. An authentic real-life community-centered approach requires development of norms for the classroom and school, as well as connections to the outside world that support core learning values, build on contributions of individual members, and confer a sense of ownership.[86]

All these implications are natural extensions from what we know how students' brains learn. These require students to take more ownership and responsibility of their own learning. The classroom needs to be a place conducive to challenge without negative stress and a place for social interaction. The student experience needs to show relevance, to be authentic, and to be contextually based. The best educators are already using many of these practices, and such teaching practices can be very rewarding. Part III will show how.

The Curriculum

The curriculum is the domain of the faculty—the experts in the content area. What we have learned about the brain will have a direct impact, however, on how experts structure what they teach, how they teach it, the work they assign, and how they assess the effectiveness of their instruction. In so doing, teachers need to help their students connect to previous learning and memories, to scaffold these experiences, and to make learning opportunities be authentic, contextual, and experiential wherever possible. Parents play a critical role at home helping their children scaffold current learning with previous experiences outside the classroom.

Well-designed learning activities do more than simply present information. They help students engage with the content and guide students to connect previous memories and experiences to help construct, scaffold, and integrate the new. We know that memory improves through practice, and therefore adults need to provide opportunities for students to practice and struggle with new concepts. The brain can memorize a great deal of information but learning through trial and error and integration is ultimately more efficient. When developing lesson plans or units of instruction, teachers should keep in mind the hierarchical levels of learning according to Bloom's Taxonomy. This will help focus the curriculum and instruction on higher-level skills and intellectual engagement.

Student learning becomes more effective as they become aware and critical of their own thinking and their previous assumptions.[87] It is imperative instructors help students incorporate metacognitive practices as part of their learning routines. As such, adults need to model their own thinking with their students and to lead them to become self-motivated—to take ownership of their own learning. In modeling, instructors show their own thinking out loud, how they grapple with subjects, and how they arrive at their well-considered decisions. Such practices mirror those attributes of critical thinking.

Certainly, one primary goal for teachers is to help students to move short-term and working memory into long-term memory. One method is for students to put into their own words, via writing, speaking, or presenting, what they have learned. In addition, while we know repetition of specific facts is a relatively ineffective way to learn, students do learn new information more easily and remember it longer when they connect it with things they already know, as well as to things that are context- and real-life-based. Further, learning is enhanced by emphasizing the big picture and then allowing students to discover the details for themselves.

Whether or not our students can attain expertise in the subject matter, we are reminded of the work by Bransford and his colleagues about characteristics of outstanding students. They have learned to notice features and meaningful patterns of information that are not recognized by novices. They have acquired a great deal of content knowledge that is organized in ways that reflect a deep understanding of their subject matter. Their knowledge cannot be reduced to sets of isolated facts or propositions but instead reflects contexts of applicability: that is, their knowledge is "conditionalized" on a set of circumstances. Finally, they can flexibly retrieve important aspects of their knowledge with little attentional effort.[88]

The most important takeaway is that educators need to help students understand the applicability of contextualized learning by seeing the whole picture first. Further, they must dive deep into the given topic to understand it thoroughly and to develop a conceptualization of patterns and relationships—to make sense of the content. Students need to realize the connections between the parts to the whole, and to see the relevance, in other words.

As students take ownership of their learning, parents and teachers alike need to keep in mind motivational principles elucidated in Maslow's Hierarchy of Needs. The focus needs to be on learning and not teaching. To paraphrase Paulo Freire, "Don't take away the dignity of their struggle."[89] The students need time to process, to reflect—to think about what they are learning. Physical space and time must be given so they can make these requisite intellectual connections and leaps.

Our best students are self-disciplined, prefer complexity and realistic activity, but enjoy high challenges, and take ownership and responsibility for their own learning. Such classroom environments and curriculum drive pedagogy of the best educators.

Pedagogy

Pedagogy is *how* we teach our content to the students. Too often, adults teach the way they were taught—their mimetic isomorphism. It's the only approach they have ever seen, so it's the only way they know how to approach their instruction. What we have learned about brain research and learning theory can change *how* we teach and help our children grow developmentally.

Contemporary learning theories and subsequent pedagogical strategies will be further developed in part II. However, some key concepts are worth exploring presently. Professors William McKeachie and Marilla Svinicki explained the proper perspective:

> What is important is learning, not teaching. Teaching effectiveness depends not just on what the teacher does, but rather on what the student does. Teaching involves listening as much as talking. It's important that both teacher and students are actively thinking, but most important is what goes on in the students' minds. Those minds are not blank slates. They hold expectations, experiences, and conceptions that will shape their interpretation of the knowledge you present. Your task is to help them develop mental representations of your subject matter that will provide a basis for further learning, thinking, and use.[90]

Robert Leamnson expressed, "If learning is indeed a matter of brain development—synapses stabilized through use—it becomes equally clear that it cannot be effected by anyone but the learner."[91] Thus, while learning causes changes in the brains—strengthens neural connections and makes memories and subsequent recall easier and more interconnected—it is the student who must take control, ownership, and ultimate responsibility for their own learning. This is certainly true for college students. In *What the Best College Professors Do*, Ken Bain concluded:

> The best college and university teachers create what we might call a natural critical learning environment in which they embed the skills and information they wish to teach in assignments . . . authentic tasks that will arouse curiosity, challenging students to rethink their assumptions and examine their mental models of reality. They create a safe environment in which students can try, come up short, receive feedback, and try again. Students understand and remember what they have learned because they master and use the reasoning abilities necessary to integrate it with larger concepts.[92]

When we teach, we need to take advantage of the unconscious mind and the inclination of emotion to engage learners and to connect with previous learning experiences and memories. We need to train students to slow down, to reflect, and to engage the executive center of their brains—to be mindful in how they approach their own learning.

Students' brains actively seek to engage the content to construct and scaffold their learning. Useful, practical, and functional knowledge is based on activity. People build new knowledge by using their brain actively to solve real-world problems or real-life situations. Since human brains are social brains, we need to take advantage of the social environment of our classrooms and create opportunities for students to work with one another whether in the classroom or outside of it.

The best instructors use differentiation in teaching strategies to deal with the various learning styles of their students. The students themselves can help do this. Students can explicitly show their peers how they approach and solve problems. In turn, students will learn a variety of ways to resolve issues and which approaches are optimal.

In addition, when a student verbalizes or puts in writing their understanding of a concept or how they solve a problem, they are forced to be clear and precise—to themselves. The feedback they receive from their classmates, indeed their own reflection, will likely force better understanding. In other words, students not only learn from each other, but they learn from themselves through the process of metacognition and explanation whether in speaking, in writing, or in action. In fact, self-talk is a common trait found in the most creative thinkers.

We need to avoid long lectures. Only 5 to 10 percent of information imparted during a lecture is retained after just one day. Discussion is a more effective way of ensuring retention. Teachers need to grab their students' attention, or at least show its relevance, within the first twenty seconds of introducing a new subject and should captivate their students with a topic that is meaningful, according to Eric Jensen and Liesl McConchie. These authors differentiate between episodic and semantic learning:

> [E]xplicit inputs are initiated by life experiences—or what we, as educators might call direct instruction. Episodic learning is usually rich in sensory information, and therefore our discussion of sensory inputs involves [various] processes, systems, and structures . . . [and] often includes the brain's emotional headquarters . . . Semantic learning, on the other hand, is often less sense-enriched unless a teacher is highly skilled in the art of differentiated instruction. A traditional lecture will only involve the language systems of and structures of the brain . . . with the occasional inclusion of visual systems and structures . . . when visual presentations are used.[93]

Cognition and memories are strengthened, as a matter of fact, by rich experiences and by activating multiple regions of the brain using the different senses. The more senses involved and the more experiences we have, the greater the ability to remember and to think at higher levels. Most learners (40 to 65 percent) would be considered visual learners, as noted earlier. Auditory learners comprise another 25 to 30 percent, and 5 to 15 percent are primarily kinesthetic learners. The more ways we can help students access our content, the more likely they will learn.

Students need to connect working memory with long-term memory by linking the present situation to past experiences. Moreover, evidence suggests the value of teaching content in small chunk sizes. Research says two to four chunks are realistic in terms of the capacity for working memory. More than that, students are unable to make the transition from the immediate memory to the long-term.

The learning task must be authentic and geared toward real-life and problem-solving activities for the students. Teaching content in isolation from reality makes understanding all the more difficult. Moreover, Piaget emphasized that the learner's brain can more readily accommodate new knowledge when it is able to reach into its stores of memories, better known as schemas, and connect the new knowledge to its preexisting knowledge. When this accommodation does not happen, mental disequilibrium ensues.

In their work published by the National Academy Press, John Bransford and his colleagues perhaps summed this section up best with "Implications for Teaching":

1. "Teachers must draw out and work with the preexisting understandings that their students bring with them. The teacher must actively inquire into students' thinking creating classroom tasks and conditions under which student thinking can be revealed. The roles for assessment must be expanded beyond the traditional concept of testing. . . . Frequent formative assessment helps make students' thinking visible to themselves and their teachers."[AQ2] Such assessments will focus more on high-order thinking and activities.
2. Teachers must focus on depth rather than breadth in their instruction. This will reach higher-level cognitive processes and learning. Assessment will subsequently take on a new focus with fewer multiple choice and other factual exams and more reality-based performance examinations. Such examinations are difficult to prepare and have a more subjective rather than objective basis.
3. Teachers must help students learn metacognitive skills so they can become independently master their own reflective practices.[94] They need to think about their own thinking, to reflect and challenge their

own assumptions, and to critically examine how they arrive at their conclusions.

Finally, the effectiveness of our teaching and the success of our students' learning needs to be measured and analyzed, or assessed, if you will. A combined strategy of formative and summative assessment of both our teaching and of the students' learning must be examined in toto.

Assessment

Summative assessment, as the name implies, is typically an evaluation given in summation or as a summary of learning at the end of a unit of study. These are often associated with formal grades and at times may be considered high stakes—to determine a student's final grade, their ability to pass a course, or as a comprehensive exam, for example.

Formative assessments are more ongoing throughout a given period, say a unit of study, and can be either formal or informal. Grades may or may not be associated with formative assessments. They are designed to quickly determine students' grasp of material, quality of instruction, and whether additional or modified instruction is necessary. Such assessments help both the instructor and the student check their progress.

In a very real sense, the ways in which teachers assess students' learning influence what and how students learn. In other words, what and how students learn depend, in part, on how they expect their learning to be assessed. Educators often hear the refrain: "Will it be on the test?" If it's not going to be on the test, less effort will be given. What gets assessed gets taught and learned. As such, teachers need to grapple with the purpose of grading. Is it to determine whether a student should successfully pass the course, or is its purpose to make teaching adjustments and provide feedback to the students, for example?

The best exams should, like assignments, be learning experiences as well as evaluative mechanisms. Educators lose valuable opportunities to advance student learning when they use a grade as merely a culminating marker. After an exam is given, there is a prime opportunity for the instructor to review the correct answers with the class. Often students will guess the answers and might get them correct without ever really knowing. Reviewing the answers is an opportunity to correct understanding and misunderstanding.

Finally, how students receive assessment feedback can be equally important. Again, they may have a fight or flight response to feedback if it is handled in a stressful manner. If this is the case, the teacher loses an opportunity for a learning experience. If students just want to get away from the feedback, they won't be in an emotional position to receive it—to learn from it. So, we need to be careful how they receive our communication; we don't want to make the students defensive. In other words, the goal is to focus on feedback as a learning experience, not simply a pro forma reporting mechanism.

Summary

In sum, the lessons we have learned about how the brain works can have significant implications for our curriculum, the way we teach, our classroom environments, and how we assess both the students' learning and the subsequent effectiveness of our instruction.

As we know, most students have a left-brain or right-brain propensity for learning, for thinking, and for processing information. As such, students prefer certain personal approaches to learning. So, too, teachers have preferred ways to teach. The best instructors find ways to reach all their learners—to differentiate their instruction.

We have learned that left-brain-dominated students are most comfortable learning through reading, writing, and speaking. They prefer linear and sequential thinking moving from parts to the whole. They need to analyze all the facts before understanding how concepts come together. They prefer structured and orderly classrooms. Left-brain educators post class agendas and teach using lecture notes and story maps. They are orderly, well-managed, and on time, and their lessons are well-structured and predictable. Conversely, right brain learners wish their teachers used illustrations and discussions.

Right-brained students are comfortable with emotions, feelings, and intuition. They learn from novel thinking. It is here where options are explored, images are visualized, and imagination is nurtured. They prefer to see things moving from the whole to the parts. They are global big picture learners. They prefer melody, pattern recognition, intuition, and spontaneity, and are tolerant of ambiguity and unpredictable situations. These educators use visuals, diagrams, and hands-on lessons, along with discussions and problem-based learning. In these classrooms, left-brain learners want more structure, organization, and predictability.[95]

Geoffrey and Renate Caine have condensed all these lessons into seven principles for application of the brain-compatible adult classroom. In part, these are[96]:

1. *Learning is collaborative and influenced by interactions with others:* The human brain is a social brain. Professors need to allow learners to select their own flexible seating with and encourage differential groupings for students to engage with one another—to learn from one

another. Interacting out loud forces students to clarify, justify, and extend their thinking.
2. *The adult brain creates meaning by linking past to present into familiar patterns:* Adult learners want to engage by actively challenging concepts to make sense of the content. This process helps them to connect to existing neural networks. The new knowledge then becomes integrated into the learner's existing knowledge and creates opportunity for scaffolding. The brain processes information both sequentially and holistically through communication between the hemispheres as the entire brain interacts as a dynamic whole.
3. *Emotions and stress can adversely impact learning:* The brain is heavily influenced by emotional stimuli. The brain makes greater synaptic connections between neurons when it is appropriately challenged with novel experiences. However, under stressful or threatening conditions, the student's brain may shift down to the primitive region where survival is the focus. As a result, learners are less likely to tap into their higher-order thinking and creativity when negative emotions surface. Educators can promote higher-level learning by encouraging self-efficacy and creating an environment of relaxed alertness, which involves low threat and high challenge.
4. *Adults learn through both conscious, focused attention and unconscious, peripheral processing:* Most learning takes place at the subconscious level. Professors need to make efforts to have students reflect upon what they have learned and to creatively elaborate on their reflections, ideas, and experiences to make the learning more meaningful. In other words, they need to help make the implicit explicit. At the same time, the brain also needs frequent breaks from direct focused attention to process information in a more effective manner. A nonstop flow of information, such as in the traditional lecture, may be counterproductive to the natural way the brain learns. Regular breaks every twenty to thirty minutes are beneficial. Opportunities to talk informally with others about what they learned is an excellent strategy.
5. *Adult learners process information through multiple memory pathways:* The best instructors encourage learners to integrate what they are learning into their own personal life experiences and then encourage learners to relate new concepts to past experiences and prerequisite knowledge. This scaffolding approach helps students to construct a comprehensive and integrated approach to learning. Eliciting emotions is a prime way to tie into previous experiences. Fortunately, adult learners enjoy a plethora of real-life prior experiences to bring to the college classroom environment. Professors need to take advantage of this.

6. *The adult brain is uniquely organized and never stops learning:* Neural plasticity is an advantage of the adult learner. Professors should use a variety of teaching modalities (auditory, visual, and kinesthetic) to help their adult students bring in previous learning and life experiences and make connections across brain networks. Giving students multiple opportunities to present their understanding of new concepts, to discuss with other students, and to create physical representations are all simple ways to support these different modes.
7. *A healthy lifestyle contributes to optimal learning:* Some of these principles are out of the instructor's control. However, professors can encourage the students to get plenty of sleep[97]—a very difficult challenge for the working professional—to get adequate physical exercise—another difficult challenge for the working adult—and to eat healthy. Perhaps the best advice is for students to be properly hydrated. Professors can support this effort by permitting students to have water in the classroom or to take routine refreshment breaks. Once students begin to show signs of distraction, it is a good time for a physical break. This allows not only a chance to stretch and get rehydrated, but it is also an opportunity to think about what has just been learned as noted in principle four.

Together, all that we have learned about the brain should have tremendous impact on how we teach our students. At the same time, educators and cognitive scientists have spent years pondering the questions about how students learn best, and in turn, how teachers should reach their students. Learning theory and cognition, the work of these considered professionals, is the focus of part II. Most interestingly, there are models, and parts of models, that are best supported by what we have learned from brain research, and together they can help students construct their own learning.

NOTES

1. Olaf Sporns, *Networks of the Brain* (Cambridge, MA: MIT Press, 2011). In terms of learning and how the brain functions,

There is no learned skill that uses only one part of the brain, and there is no one part of the brain with a singular function. Instead, the brain systems that support learning and academic skills are the same brain systems that are integral to personhood—that is, to social, cognitive, emotional, and cultural functioning and even to health and physiological survival.

Mary Helen Immordino-Yang and Rebecca Gotlieb, "Embodied Brains, Social Minds, Cultural Meaning: Integrating Neuroscientific and Educational Research on

Social-Affective Development," *American Educational Research Journal: Centennial Issue* 54, 1 (2017): 344S–367S, cited in Institute of Medicine, *From Neurons to Neighborhoods: The Science of Early Childhood Development* (Washington, DC: National Academy Press, 2000).

2. Richard Restak, *The New Brain: How the Modern Age is Rewiring Your Brain* (Emmaus, PA: Rodale Press, 2003): 125. Restack goes on to note: "Rather than the gene itself, the ultimate determiner of genetic fate is the network of connections and reactions within the cell," (125). It is not a matter of good or bad genes, but rather the networks interacting with one another throughout the brain.

3. Jane Healy, *Your Child's Growing Mind: Brain Development and Learning from Birth to Adolescence* (New York: Broadway Books, 2007): 8.

4. Institute of Medicine, *From Neurons to Neighborhoods: The Science of Early Childhood Development* (Washington, DC: National Academy Press, 2000); National Academies of Sciences, Engineering, and Medicine, *How People Learn II: Learners, Contexts, and Cultures* (Washington, DC: The National Academies Press, 2018), 56, cited research of the National Research Council and Institute of Medicine, *Transforming the Workforce for Children Birth Through Age 8: A Unifying Foundation* (Washington, DC: The National Academies Press, 2015), and Gerry Leisman, Raed Mualem, and Safa Khayat Mughrabi, "The Neurological Development of the Child with the Educational Enrichment in Mind" *Psicología Educativa* 21, no. 2 (2015): 79–96. Among the key findings of early brain development and its effects on lifelong learning:

Experience and genetics both contribute to observed variability in human development. The human brain develops from conception through the early 20s and beyond in an orderly progression. Vital and autonomic functions develop first, then cognitive, motor, sensory, and perceptual processes, with complex integrative processes and value-driven and long-term decision making developing last. Early adversity can have important short- and long-term effects on the brain's development and other essential functions.

5. Rhosel Lenroot and Jay Giedd, "Brain Development in Children and Adolescents: Insights from Anatomical Magnetic Resonance Imaging," *Neuroscience Biobehavioral Review* 30, no. 6 (2006): 718–29.

6. Robert Sylwester, *A Celebration of Neurons: An Educator's Guide to the Human Brain* (Alexandria, VA: Association of Supervision and Curriculum Development, 1995), 127–28.

7. Healy, Your Child's Growing Mind, 79: "Youngsters in well-structured 'play'-oriented preschools and developmentally appropriate primary grades develop more positive attitudes toward learning along with better ultimate skill development" (as opposed to primarily academic-focused schools). Healy adds that kindergarten teachers look to see if the student can communicate their thoughts and needs, is enthusiastic and curious, follows directions, and socializes well with peers (88).

8. Eric Jensen and Liesl McConchie, *Brain-Based Learning: Teaching the Way Students Really Learn* (Thousand Oaks, CA: Corwin, 2020), 16. Jensen and McConchie elaborated on the systems involved in healthy brain functioning by including

digestive, respiratory, nervous, circulatory, and sympathetic and parasympathetic systems (15).

9. Sylwester, *A Celebration of Neurons*, 27.

10. Sylwester, *A Celebration of Neurons*, 75.

11. John Medaglia, Mary-Ellen Lynall, and Danielle Bassett, "Cognitive Network Neuroscience," *Journal of Cognitive Neuroscience* 27, no. 8 (2015): 1471–91.

12. Healy, *Your Child's Growing Mind*, 20.

13. Healy, *Your Child's Growing Mind*, 230. For example, the limbic system, the hippocampus, the amygdala, and the cerebral cortex all play critical roles in memory depending on the type of stimulus.

14. Sylwester, *A Celebration of Neurons*, 89.

15. Healy, *Your Child's Growing Mind*, 232–33. Memories are best created when children are actively engaged in the experience and talk about it both contemporaneously and by recall.

16. Michio Kaku, *The Future of the Mind: The Scientific Quest to Understand, Enhance, and Empower the Mind* (New York: Doubleday, 2014), 123–24.

17. National Academies, *How People Learn II*, 75.

18. Mihalyi Csikszentmihalyi, *Flow: The Psychology of Optimal Experience* (New York: Harper Collins, 1990), 26.

19. Daniel Levitin, *This is Your Brain on Music: The Science of a Human Obsession* (New York: Plume of Penguin Group, 2006), 57. Levitin adds: "Musical activity involves nearly every region of the brain that we know about, and nearly every neural subsystem" (85–86).

20. Laurie Materna, *Jump Start the Adult Learner: How to Engage and Motivate Adults Using Brain-Compatible Strategies* (Thousand Oaks, CA: Corwin Press, 2007): 3–9. A brief and very generalized paraphrased description of the brain systems follows. Much greater detail is provided later in the part along with implications for educators.

The lower brain is made up of the brain stem and the cerebellum. This is the brain's first region to mature and is primarily responsible for survival, for much of our sensory data, for basic bodily regulation, for motor movement, and to communicate with the middle brain, among other responsibilities. Should a person perceive threats to their survival, impulses to the lower brain will not continue to move to the more advanced areas of the brain—indeed, classroom learning will likely not occur.

The middle brain is made up of the limbic system: amygdala, hippocampus, and the thalamus. It is known as the portion of the brain regulating hormones and our emotions. It communicates with the thinking part of the brain as well as the motor part. Our senses, with the exception of smell, are regulated here, and many of our memories are stored here. Much of our short-term memories, working knowledge, and attention are stored and activated in the middle brain. This region of the brain works with the prefrontal cortex to determine the response to stimuli found by our senses and to our emotions.

The upper brain is made up of the cerebrum and is covered by the neocortex. This is the last portion of the brain to develop and is where most of our thinking is done. It is divided into two hemispheres and four lobes: frontal, occipital, parietal, and temporal.

The two hemispheres are connected by a thick nerve fiber—the corpus callosum—which serves as the communication link between the hemispheres and the lobes. While each hemisphere and each lobe have primary functions, each is intimately integrated with one another. No thinking is done without the interactions of the others.

21. Colin Rose, *Accelerated Learning Action Guide* (Aylesbury Buckinghamshire, UK: Accelerated Learning Systems, 1995). This document was cited in Materna, *Jump Start the Adult Learner*, 29.

22. Healy, *Your Child's Growing Mind*, 372.

23. Kaku, *The Future of the Mind*, 220.

24. Neurotransmitters are natural chemicals which include dopamine, serotonin, and norepinephrine.

25. Materna, *Jump Start the Adult Learner*, 24. Materna added a hopeful insight:

the brain not only creates new cells, throughout a lifetime but . . . the new cells live longer and grow stronger when the brain is actively engaged in new learning. This research is particularly exciting in terms of adult learning and supports the need for promoting learning activities that naturally engage adults' motivation, interests, and attention by drawing upon personal experiences. (24)

26. National Academies, *How People Learn II*, 4.

27. Sylwester, *A Celebration of Neurons*, 89.

28. Restak, *The New Brain*, 32.

29. Evan Thompson, *Waking, Dreaming, Being: Self and Consciousness in Neuroscience, Meditation, and Philosophy* (New York: Columbia University Press, 2017), 342, 343.

30. Michael Talbot, *The Holographic Universe* (New York: Harper Collins, 1991), 20.

31. Sylwester, *A Celebration of Neurons*, 120.

32. Healy, *Your Child's Growing Mind*, 35. Healy continued:

Studies show that children who are heavily managed by caregivers may lack both initiative and thinking skills. When adults are overly restrictive in controlling . . . children show up with poorer problem-solving skills, mental organization, and motivation. . . . Be sensitive to nature's automatic shut-off valve, the signs of overexcitement or crankiness which show that the child has had enough. Exhaustion, anxiety, pressure, or fear make it impossible for the neurons to send or receive the desired figures. (38)

33. Healy, *Your Child's Growing Mind*, 41, 50.

34. [AQ1]

35. Jeanne Ellis Ormrod and Brett Jones, *Essentials of Educational Psychology* (New York: Pearson, 2019), 210. The authors elaborate:

In the cortex—and especially the prefrontal cortex—synaptic pruning continues into the middle childhood and adolescent years, a second wave of synaptogenesis occurs at puberty, and myelination continues into early adulthood. And several parts of the brain, especially those that are heavily involved in thinking and learning, continue to increase in size and interconnections until late adolescence or early adulthood. (211)

36. National Academies, *How People Learn II*, 70.

37. Levitin, *This is Your Brain on Music*, 185.
38. Sylwester, *A Celebration of Neurons*, 95.
39. Andrew Holecek, *Dream Yoga: Illuminating Your Life through Lucid Dreaming and the Tibetan Yogas of Sleep* (Boulder, CO: Sounds True, 2016).
40. Materna, *Jump Start the Adult Learner*. For greater detail to the discussion of the lower, middle, and upper portions of the brain and implications for educational practices, the reader is invited to read part 1 of Materna's book.
41. Materna, *Jump Start the Adult Learner*, 34.
42. Sylwester, *A Celebration of Neurons*, 113. In other words, emotions take precedence unless we purposefully take the time to reflect and be judicial.
43. Fred Alan Wolf, *The Dreaming Universe: A Mind-Expanding Journey into the Realm Where Psyche and Physics Meet* (New York: Touchstone of Simon and Schuster, 1994), 96.
44. Materna, *Jump Start the Adult Learner*, 8. Materna adds that the hippocampus works with factual, or semantic, memories, while the amygdala is responsible for memories associated with our emotions. Healy, *Your Child's Growing Mind*, 243, further explained: "The hippocampus mediates factual memory and the amygdala attaches emotional significance to experience so that we can quickly classify a stimulus as potentially dangerous." Thus, "the limbic system, can either facilitate learning or block the thinking systems."
45. Institute of Medicine, *From Neurons to Neighborhoods: The Science of Early Childhood Development* (Washington, DC: National Academy Press, 2000).
46. Ormrod and Jones, *Essentials of Educational Psychology*, 23.
47. Jensen and McConchie, *Brain-Based Learning*, 102.
48. Ormrod and Jones, *Essentials of Educational Psychology*, 22. According to the authors, the prefrontal cortex doesn't reach maturity until humans reach their early twenties (210).
49. Bloom's Taxonomy of Learning is discussed in detail in part III.
50. Sylwester, *A Celebration of Neurons*, 54.
51. Holecek, *Dream Yoga*, 272.
52. For a detailed yet erudite explanation of how the system of neurons interconnect as individual pieces to form into a cogent understanding of a full picture or understanding, the reader is encouraged to read Sylwester, *A Celebration of Neurons*, part 2.
53. Materna, *Jump Start the Adult Learner*, 22.
54. Douglas Hacker, "Failures to Detect Textual Problems during Reading," in *Processing Inaccurate Information: Theoretical and Implied Perspectives from Cognitive Science and the Educational Sciences*, edited by David Rapp and Jason Braasch (Cambridge, MA: The MIT Press, 2014), 88.
55. Sylwester, *A Celebration of Neurons*, 49.
56. Ormrod and Jones, *Essentials of Educational Psychology*, 22.
57. Materna, *Jump Start the Adult Learner*, 14.
58. Kaku, *The Future of the Mind*, 37. With regard to left-brain dominance, Kaku expresses an interesting take on brain injuries and on autistic behavior. "Normally, the left brain restricts this talent [the creative side of the right brain] and holds it

in check. But if the left brain is injured in a certain way, it may unleash the artistic abilities latent in the right brain, causing an explosion of artistic talent" (145). Others have speculated that certain drugs may inhibit the dominant authority of the left brain, providing opportunity for artistic expression. Others have even suggested that the left side of the brain becomes less dominant when we sleep, which allows more right brain activity, hence stranger dreams.

59. Healy, *Your Child's Growing Mind*, 261. To which Healy added: "The time you spend reading to your child is the best predictor of later reading success" (266).

60. Holecek, *Dream Yoga*, 14. Holecek went on to note:

Researchers at Georgetown University discovered that during naps, the right hemisphere of the brain, which is associated with creativity, is very active, while the left hemisphere, which is more analytical, is relatively quiet. The left hemisphere, which tends to dominate the right, specializes in numbers and language processing. It's almost as if when the chattering and reasoning left hemisphere shuts up, the creative right hemisphere opens up. (14)

61. Leonard Shlain, *The Alphabet Versus the Goddess: The Conflict Between Word and Image* (New York: Penguin Group, 1998), 17, 23.

62. Restak, *The New Brain*, 72, for example expressed,

If you're driving in unfamiliar surroundings while glancing down at a map, it's primarily your right hemisphere that processes the lines and figures on the map. Bit if, instead, someone in the passenger seat is telling you directions, your left hemisphere is the primary processor of the verbal description of your route. (72)

63. Healy, *Your Child's Growing Mind*, 336.

64. Yongman Chang, "Reorganization and Plastic Changes of the Human Brain Associated with Skill Learning and Expertise," *Frontiers in Human Neuroscience* 8, no. 35 (2014); Sara Bengtsson, Zoltan Nagy, Stefan Skare, Lea Forsman, Hans Forssberg, and Fredrik Ullen, "Extensive Piano Practicing Has Regionally Specific Effects on White Matter Development," *Nature Neuroscience* 8 no. 9 (2005): 1148–50.

65. John Bransford, Ann Brown, and Rodney Cocking, eds., *How People Learn: Brain, Mind, Experience, and School* (Washington, DC: National Academy Press, 2000), 31.

Often, experts are considered expert in their field because of their vast experience in the content field, besides their high degree of training. In addition, "Experts look for patterns and chunk information. . . . They organize key concepts around big ideas and concepts and relationships—part of chunking, look at alternative solutions" (36).

66. Healy, *Your Child's Growing Mind*, 351–52.

67. Sylwester, *A Celebration of Neurons*, 112.

68. Levitin, *This is Your Brain on Music*, 125. Levitin added: "The front portion of the corpus callosum . . . is significantly larger in musicians than nonmusicians. . . . This reinforces the notion that musical operations become bilateral with increased training, as musicians coordinate and recruit neural structures in both the left and right hemispheres" (226).

69. Restak, *The New Brain*, 4.

70. Restak, *The New Brain*, 24–26.

71. Restak, *The New Brain*, 14. The reader is invited to a fascinating read of part 2—"Genius and Superior Performance: Are We All Capable?"—of Restak's book as it is devoted to an exhaustive study of genius musicians, chess masters, athletes, and others.

72. Restak, *The New Brain*, 15. Restak believes, among other researchers, that expertise is less a matter of innate qualities, and more a matter of hard work, determination, focus, and the ability to self-direction and self-control. They[AQ3] are flexible in their thinking and problem-solving and are constantly seeking to improve. They are their own best or toughest judges. Like Healy, Materna, and others, Restak cites those with superior performance exhibiting traits of "flow," as coined by Mihalyi Cziskzentmihalyi.

73. Restak, *The New Brain*, 21. Restak went on to explain similar attributes in musicians: "Musically sophisticated individuals are more likely to perceive music in an analytical manner and thus rely more heavily on their dominant (usually left) hemisphere" (98).

74. Gail Davies, Max Lam, Sarah Harris, Joey Trampush, Michelle Luciano, and W. David Hill, "Study of 300,486 Individuals Identifies 148 Independent Genetic Loci Influencing General Cognitive Function," *Nature Communications* 9, no. 1 (2018): 1–16.

75. David Bueno, "Genetics and Learning: How the Genes Influence Educational Attainment," *Frontiers in Psychology* 10 (2019): 1–10.

76. Kaili Rimfeld, Z. Ayorech, P. Dale, Y. Kovas, and R. Plomin, "Genetics Affects Choice of Academic Subjects as well as Achievement," *Scientific Reports* 6 (2016): 1–9.

77. Bueno, "Genetics and Learning," 7.

78. Bueno, "Genetics and Learning."

79. Sylwester, *A Celebration of Neurons*, 129–30.

80. Jensen and McConchie, *Brain-Based Learning*, 86.

81. Jensen and McConchie, *Brain-Based Learning*, 102. They concluded, "Your students' brains will naturally prioritize emotional processes over academic content. Students who are preoccupied with something emotional, not related to the learning, will struggle" (103). Wolf drove home the critical necessity of emotions to learning: "Feelings create emotions, and emotions are vital to having any memory at all. In other words, we do not remember anything that we have no feelings about." Fred Alan Wolf, *The Dreaming Universe: A Mind-Expanding Journey into the Realm Where Psyche and Physics Meet* (New York: Touchstone, 1994), 45.

82. Healy, *Your Child's Growing Mind*.

83. Materna, *Jump Start the Adult Learner*. "All in all, whole-brain learning uses the creative-intuitive mind as well as the critical-logical mind to accomplish a variety of learning goals" (19).

84. Jensen and McConcchie, *Brain-Based Learning*, 147–48. To which they added:

Three factors that operate at non-conscious level that are needed for optimal brain performance and learning: 1) Safety, 2) Belonging, 3) Hope and support. Students who have a sense of belonging to a school or classroom community are more likely to engage in positive academic behaviors that produce higher levels of engagement and performance. And Do I fit in? Do people care about me? Am I valued? (152)

85. Zaretta Hammond, *Culturally Responsive Teaching and the Brain: Promoting Authentic Engagement and Rigor among Culturally and Linguistically Diverse Sstudents* (New York: Corwin Press, 2015).

86. Bransford, Brown, and Cocking, *How People Learn*, 23–25.

87. Levitin, *This is Your Brain on Music*, 105. The brain makes errors, so students need to confront their previous understandings and to correct where needed. According to Levitin: "The brain constructs a representation of reality, based on . . . component features. . . . In the process, the brain makes a number of inferences, due to incomplete or ambiguous information; sometimes these inferences turn out to be wrong" (105). Initially, the professor can help students reflect upon previous understanding and assumptions. Eventually, students can learn metacognitive practices in order to deconstruct faulty learning so they can then construct new learning upon a sound foundation.

88. Bransford, Brown, and Cocking, *How People Learn*, 31.

89. Paulo Freire, *Pedagogy of the Oppressed* (New York: Continuum International Publishing, 1970).

90. Wilbert McKeachie and Marilla Svinicki, *Teaching Tips: Strategies, Research, and Theory for College and University Teachers* (Boston: Houghton-Mifflin, 2006), 6.

91. Robert Leamnson, *Thinking about Teaching and Learning: Developing Habits of Learning with First Year College and University Students* (Sterling, VA: Sylus Publishing, 1999), 18.

92. Ken Bain, *What the Best College Teachers Do* (Cambridge, MA: Harvard University Press, 2004), 47.

93. Jensen and McConchie, *Brain-Based Learning*, 24–25.

94. Bransford, Brown, and Cocking, *How People Learn*, 19–21. Paraphrased by the authors of this book.

95. Materna, *Jump Start the Adult Learner*, 15–16. These descriptions of left- and right-brain students and teachers are paraphrased from the work of Materna.

96. Renate Nummela and Geoffrey Caine, *Understanding a Brain-Based Approach to Learning and Teaching* (Alexandria, VA: Educational Leadership, Association for Supervision and Curriculum Development, 1990), 66–70. The text in italics comes from the source, while the text that follows it is combined paraphrasing and commentary of the authors of this book.

97. "Activation of the hippocampus (which plays a key role in memory integration) during sleep seems to allow connections between memory traces to be formed across the cortex." National Academies, *How People Learn II*, 87.

Part II

Learning Theory

Whose knowledge is of most worth, and how do we construct a society that reproduces such knowledge? This question has been probed, pondered, and tested since the beginning of humanity, as we continuously strive to assimilate into ways of knowing, norms, institutions, and careers that fulfill them. Through storytelling, imitation, paintings, and field experience, humans have learned methods to survive, build, and prosper. In other words, learning has always been a component of our very nature.

Therefore, it is always a critical social priority to instill in our youth values that we have wanted to reproduce to ensure our continued progression. Thus, to question whose knowledge is of most worth and how we reproduce such knowledge is to inquire about learning and establishing structures that foster children's ability to learn. In part II, we will discuss perspectives on learning from ancient civilizations, the effects of both nature and nurture, the most practiced learning theories from the twenty-first century, and, lastly, implications for supporting students both in the classroom and at home.

ANCIENT PERSPECTIVES ON LEARNING

Ancient perspectives on learning have offered educators a great deal of material to learn from. Upon studying academia in environments from thousands of years ago, one notices that many of the approaches to learning are similar to what we do today and how we have come to understand which strategies work best to teach children. Therefore, in this section, we will briefly explore ancient perspectives on teaching children, which essentially included community building, strategic role modeling, and imagination.

Khety of Ancient Egypt and Precolonial Africa

During the twelfth dynasty of ancient Egyptian civilization, the teachings of Dua Khety became popular. Khety created a composition to teach his son what he viewed as essential knowledge before he started school.[1] He instructed his son to have a positive and respectful attitude toward learning.[2] Khety explained, "love the books like your mother."[3] Because Khety's lectures to his son emphasized the importance of an educated society, his teachings later became a component of the ancient Egyptian teaching and learning philosophy.[4] It provided a blueprint for societal duty (which included writing proficiency and loyalty), and students acquired it through writing practice and rote memorization.[5] Education to ancient Egyptians was critical as they believed it was necessary during life and the afterlife.[6]

Therefore, education was offered to all and in modes that served specific groups of individuals for the societal duties that they would go on to fulfill. Egyptian education was even offered to prospective leaders of foreign nations because of its rigor and formality. School hours lasted for a good portion of the day, as they do presently, and offered an extensive recess period to offer children a break in learning. Learning included reading, writing, math, science, history, music, swimming, and morals. Additionally, it included learning experiences that were like what students would experience in their prospective career fields, as well as direct lecturing.[7]

Skipping ahead many centuries, various teaching approaches existed in precolonial Africa. In some locations, teaching took place in formal systems, and in others, education took place within the many diverse life experiences that an individual would undergo. In the Nupe and Ashanti communities of West Africa, teaching occurred in formal arrangements where students learned knowledge that was considered valuable by the influential members of those societies.[8] The knowledge of most worth was medicinal, hunting, and metalworking through pedagogical approaches that included theory and practice and utilized poetry and music to engage the learners.

Initiation ceremonies of the Poro community, which upheld and celebrated community norms and societal expectations, were also part of the formal curriculum as students prepared for observances. Additionally, initiation ceremonies were done as culminating events for career training. Students would enter school as an initiation training program to prepare for specific careers in farming, security, history keeping, housekeeping, and fishing. This training could last for months to years but was specialized for the work that the child would go on to do.[9]

Other types of education in West Africa featured students learning from the adults in their households who modeled expectations in an early form of cognitivism. Parents were the primary teachers, as were generally all adults within the community.[10] These ancient peoples' approaches were prescient for today's modern pedagogy. As mentioned in part I, the brain constantly monitors the environment for stimuli. It often takes in what is happening around it with plans on imitating the action to learn what happened.

This type of learning, which included aspects such as self-control and courage, was also an early form of behaviorism as students would watch adults, mimic them, and repeat the imitation to lock it into their long-term memory. The adults intentionally designed this type of learning. Additionally, songs and play were infused into the daily learning approaches to teach cultural values and stimulate mental cognition.

Confucius, 551–479 BCE

Confucius, often regarded as a star in educational thought, emerged during the Zhou dynasty, a period of ancient China that underwent significant political and philosophical ferment. His teachings revolved around the profound concepts of Tao and Li, but he emphasized what individuals could exert control over: their morals and ethical behavior. For Confucius, the essence of education lay in the cultivation of personal character, which he believed should be grounded in the fundamental tenets of doing what is right and striving to be a "gentleman."[11] To him, being a gentleman encompassed acting with courage, fearlessness, and a commitment to goodness in all aspects of life.

Confucius encouraged his students to follow "the way," a path of moral and ethical righteousness that not only guided their behavior but also influenced their interactions with others.[12] Fundamental to his educational philosophy was the need to memorize the traditions, rituals, poetry, and songs that captured the wisdom and values of the past, thus facilitating their transmission to future generations.

Another cornerstone of Confucian educational thought was a sincere promotion of harmony.[13] He emphasized the importance of recognizing one's position and staying within the confines of one's social lane. This hierarchical structure, in Confucius's view, was pivotal for maintaining peace, understanding, and unity within society. By adhering to one's role and respecting the roles of others, individuals can foster a sense of order and balance that contributes to the overall well-being of the community.

Therefore, schools were to be fashioned with such an underpinning. It was essential to maintain peace by stratifying society into purposeful and identifiable roles supported by a poetic curriculum. Essentially, learning and teaching hinged on passing on the old ways and promoting humility to sustain society as it used artistic vehicles to engage the students.

Socrates, 469–399 BCE

Socrates, a philosopher of educational thought transcending every century of education as we know it, is known for his revolutionary philosophies that fostered critical thinking and relentless questioning. During his time in ancient Greece, Socrates pursued discovering the truth about life's questions through inquiry and introspection. He and his students questioned each other as the process to learn.

Learning, especially learning which they believed was anchored in discovery and demystifying the meaning of life, was accurately accomplished when it included interrogation. Questioning was a method to delve deeper into one's thinking. The more you realized what you did not know, the more of an effective thinker you were, according to Socrates. This fundamental aspect of Socratic education laid the groundwork for a transformative approach to learning that remains influential to this day.

This questioning that was done in the pursuit of knowledge became known as the Socratic method, and it is quite often used in the educational field. Although it is not one of the traditional learning approaches, it is popular in schools that promote inquiry-based learning, learning through speculation, and analytical processing.

Socrates believed that true learning could not be achieved by merely depositing information into students' minds like simple bank deposit transactions but, instead, by extracting, challenging, and stretching the knowledge (already formed beliefs and ideas) that resided within them.[14] Therefore, to him, learning was only possible by connecting with one's preexisting knowledge and teasing through it to bring about new meaning because they had to confront their inner conflicts on ... well ... everything that they thought was true.

Questions such as "What is the source of my beliefs?" and "Are my beliefs contradictory?" and "Which ones are more important?" encouraged deep introspection. This frequently is more engaging and thought-provoking for the brain because it irritates and engages preexisting neuronal connections, but overall is what educators today would refer to as a productive struggle.[15] Not everyone in Socrates's community appreciated this constant questioning. He was disruptive to many because he challenged dominant norms. However, his form of education had a significant influence on the world of learning. We will discuss this notion later in part II, as it appears regularly as a premise for many other learning theories, such as cognitivism and constructivism.

Plato, 429–347 BCE

Plato, another significant figure in the early school of learning and knowing, left a substantial mark on the education world and, inevitably, the US public school system through his insightful philosophies and educational principles. At the core of Plato's learning philosophy was his persistent battle against the Sophists, a group of teachers who believed that learning was subjective and contingent upon the learner's reality.[16] This starkly contrasted with Plato's understanding of knowledge, which was that knowledge was objective and not as malleable as the Sophists proclaimed. Plato promoted the idea of universal truths of facts and that education should primarily focus on searching for facts to explain life.

Plato's educational methods were bolstered by his understanding that universals truths could be unearthed through mathematic and metaphysical principles. He emphasized that students must learn these disciplines so that they would gain logical reasoning skills, which would help them realize universal truths and thereby understand the meaning of their lives.

He wanted learning to be meaningful, believing that our individual souls were important. But his interpretation of what humans needed to know was their discovery of themselves through reflection and learning math and science (i.e., his version of factual knowledge). This led students to discover shared conceptions of what mattered, what was beautiful, and ultimately what was the truth to improve society.

Aristotle, 384–322 BCE

Aristotle, a highly influential figure of learning theory and educational principles, as well as a student of Plato, continued the pursuit of examining how knowledge could be transferred and which knowledge was most worth teaching. Like everyone before him, he was fascinated with understanding how to teach, how to learn, and what was most worth knowing. In other words, what was the truth about life?

Additionally, while Aristotle was concerned about universal truths like his teachers, he was also one of the earliest pioneers of understanding social influences on learning and that, ultimately, universal truths could be agreed upon and decided by society. So there were scientifically sound truths, but also truths that groups of people could negotiate.[17]

Negotiated truths could come through persuasive language and rhetoric. Aristotle had a deep understanding of the power of language and its potential for symbolism, reasoning, and community. Language operates as a medium of cultural agreement and can be intuitively used by people as a platform to bring about new understandings. Essentially, when persuasively used, language could be used by teachers, politicians, and any leader to persuade individuals into learning, believing, and formulating shared truths.[18]

In the schools, Aristotle emphasized a structured learning environment divided into three grade bands contingent upon age essentially: primary, compulsory, and secondary for students aged seven to twenty-one. The curriculum featured a diverse range of disciplines, including music, gymnastics, drawing, literature, and math.

At higher levels of education, deductive reasoning in different disciplines continued to be the priority, though it has been noted that these levels of higher education needed to be more inclusive. However, the approach to pedagogy has been exceedingly influential in teaching approaches today. His contributions to education include persuasive writing and deductive reasoning, but also nuanced thoughts of what knowledge is worth teaching and worth knowing in the forms of curricula, state standards, and standardized testing.

Implications of Ancient Perspectives on Learning

This section has discussed the historically enduring question of whose knowledge is of most worth and how it should be transmitted to children. We have discussed ancient Egyptian and precolonial teaching models, Confucian educational philosophy, Socratic questioning, Plato's emphasis on universal truths, and Aristotle's examination of knowledge, social influences, and the role of language in forming shared truths.

We have also highlighted that various historical approaches have shaped educational environments, from formal systems to informal learning experiences. By illustrating the evolving nature of education and providing a foundation for understanding the complexities of pedagogy and knowledge, this historical context sets the stage for further exploration of diverse learning theories and developmental milestones in part II.

LEARNING AND NATURE VERSUS NURTURE

"The relationship between the individual and the environment is so extensive that it almost overstates the distinction between the two to speak of a relationship at all."[19] The body is in a constant state of communication with what is going on outside of it as it processes vast amounts of information very swiftly. Psychologists at the Massachusetts Institute of Technology estimate that the brain processes information at a speed of sixty bits per second.[20] If you tried to convert that to computer speed, it's roughly seven megabytes per second. So basically, all day, every day, our learning hinges on what is happening around us.

Incoming information is essentially software to our genetic hardware, and the two interact with each other to figure things out, make memories, and act. Human infants exhibit remarkable abilities in recognizing voices and relationships within the first few days of birth, aided by the intense acoustic signals of the mother's voice while they are in the amniotic environment. They can even differentiate the language their mother speaks during pregnancy from other languages.

This prenatal familiarity is supplemented by extensive early postnatal exposure, making the mother's voice the most consistent stimulus during the child's extended sensory-dependent development. Infants also display early sensory sensitivity to social stimuli visually, showing a preference for human faces and selectively focusing on them. By fourteen days of age, infants prefer looking at their mother's face over that of a stranger. These innate social-sensory tendencies, coupled with the intense pre- and postnatal social-sensory experiences, establish a mutual nature versus nurture relationship that regulates babies' development.[21]

The constant processing of gazes, sleep patterns, facial expressions, sounds, and rhythms have long-lasting effects on what the child perceives as usual and how they learn what is normal in their world. Wexler states that "these processes are the basis for the long-lasting effects of the social environment on the development of the human brain, the sensitivity of humans to changes in their environment in general, and their social environment in particular, and the outstanding efforts humans will make to maintain constancy in their environments."[22]

External Stimuli

The brain depends on environmental input and its sensory stimulation to maintain structural integrity. Research studies have shown that when the brain is not stimulated, or when there is a decrease in sensory input, cells in the relevant regions of the brain are reduced or pruned.

Experiments have shown that animals raised in impoverished environments have smaller brains than those without because there is less neuronal communication. As a person ages, their frontal and parietal brain lobes mature until around their third decade of life. This implies that a child's brain grows with the environmental influences that they are exposed to as neurons communicate with each other to respond to the environmental stimuli.

The brain must receive stimulating and relevant input to make new productive neuronal connections. Hammond argues that young learners become dependent learners when they are in environments that do not stimulate them in ways that are relevant to making new connections, causing a great deal of stress and anxiety as they struggle with specific learning tasks. Therefore, it is essential "to create the right instructional conditions that stimulate neuron growth and myelination by giving students work that is relevant and focused on problem-solving."[23] This can help students to not become dependent learners relying on someone to teach them.

Wexler informed us what we know about neuronal communication and how we learn by stating that our memories represent "patterned associations between neurons, caused by a permanent modification of synapses, and spreading throughout an extensive region."[24] These memories and learned ideas can be created from only a fraction of information. "This aspect of brain development is not predicated on an inborn or preexisting correspondence between the brain and the external world, but through this development, the brain is altered to bring about such a correspondence."[25]

Therefore, when children come across stimuli, the stimuli, or new thing that they are experiencing, only needs to partially resemble something that they have already experienced. Their brains will still be able to integrate and connect the new stimuli to a memory which they already had.

PARENTAL STIMULI

Parents play a crucial role in developing their babies' regulation of stimulation. This is done through various actions such as speaking in calming or exciting ways, adjusting the baby's position, providing nourishment and tactile stimulation through breastfeeding and skin-to-skin contact, and employing repetitive and familiar touch and movement.[26] These forms of involvement also aid infants in returning to equilibrium following stressful events.

Parents learn to recognize early signs of infant distress and respond with comforting measures, stimulating neural activity in the infant and helping them to restore equilibrium. With repeated parental responses, especially during moments of early distress, the babies' neural reactions to calming become quicker and stronger. As a result, the onset of distress itself can trigger the neural processes associated with self-regulation, leading to the development of self-regulatory abilities in the infant.

In other words, the adult responds to the baby's stimulus, and the baby responds to the adult's stimulus in an interrelated pattern that builds foundational interactions and learning connections between them. As these interactions become more consistent, the baby becomes accustomed to a standard, and this standard is what is needed to keep them in a state of equilibrium. Therefore, it is essential to consider children's infantile connections with environmental stimuli.

The environmental patterns that the child becomes accustomed to serve to make thick neuronal connections which are necessary for the child to continue to learn and develop. Parents also play a role in what the baby pays attention to. Often, in infancy and early childhood, the child will pay attention to what the adult prioritizes. Wexler states, "By 6 months of age, more than half of infants will follow their mother's gaze, and by the time they are a year old, nearly all will do so."[27]

Furthermore, Wexler maintains that through such means, parents influence what in the continuous stream of sensory input infants are most aware of, become most familiar with, and think most about. When the babies begin to pay attention to what the adult has deemed necessary, neuronal connections for less emphasized images are not formed in such a robust manner. As a result, the self-regulation of attention varies from person to person, culture to culture, and historical moment to historical moment.

Learning Stages and Culture

Studies have attempted to explore cultural differences in achieving the four cognitive development stages described by Jean Piaget.[28] Piaget believed that learning occurs through four stages, which he termed sensorimotor, preoperational, concrete operational, and formal operational. These stages, which he concluded through observational analyses, led him to argue that as a child grows, their ability to think becomes more abstract, and their ability to think about what they know and don't know becomes more apparent to them as they continue to interact with their environment.

Initially, it was believed that Piaget's sequence of cognitive development reflected an innate biological process that could be influenced by education and cultural context. However, these types of studies faced challenges because the tests and observational analyses that were used to conclude children's learning stages were culturally specific rather than universal measures of neurocognitive abilities.[29]

Different assessments yielded varying results, depending on the cultural background of the individuals being observed and tested. This indicates that culture profoundly influences children's abilities to recognize, understand, approach, and perform tasks. Immigrants to new countries often encounter difficulties thinking and functioning within a new cultural environment as the cognitive operations required to solve particular problems are activated in culturally specific ways. This would adversely impact testing results and cloud judgments of student intelligence.

Imitation

Imitation also plays a crucial nurturing role in the development of our brains. The strong and extended bond between parents and children, combined with the prolonged period of postnatal brain development, allows imitation to have a noteworthy impact on human growth. Imitation can be seen as a fundamental process akin to the stimulus-seeking and curiosity discussed earlier. It shapes the infant brain by absorbing the features, structures, and behaviors exhibited by adults in their regular interactions with the infant and others.

The most significant individuals that influence a child's sensory experience are their parents or primary caregivers, as well as siblings to a lesser degree. Teachers are the second most influential individuals.[30] Children imitate various aspects of these figures, including their attention, emotions, thoughts, organization of the world and self, self-perception, and actions.[31] These influential figures also provide a baseboard for the child to mix their developing motor and perceptual skills into larger behavioral patterns, thereby shaping their memories and routines. The cumulative result of these experiences is the internalization or identification of qualities resembling those of their prominent figures.

Imitation also plays a vital role in the development of language. Although the capacity to effectively use words of a specific language is connected to genetic pre-wirings, the actual language learned by infants is based on what they hear and imitate. Infants initially babble using sounds from various languages, but they eventually lose the ability to produce sounds they haven't heard before or imitated. Cases of children raised in social isolation demonstrate that without exposure to speech and the opportunity to imitate, the ability to speak and comprehend language does not develop.

Sigmund Freud noted that conflicts among different identifications that children experience as they try on new hats, imitating others, are not necessarily unreasonable. Erickson viewed such personality changes as crucial developmental occurrences of adolescence because the point here is to observe others, learning their behaviors to try out different identities until, essentially, an inner identity resonates and sticks.[32]

Social influences such as media imagery, trends, and friend groups play a significant role during this process as adolescents struggle to integrate their identifications with societal norms and available social roles. They continuously try to establish where they can and should fit in. In this journey, individuals choose an ideology from those presented by society, seeking correspondence between their inner and outer worlds while constructing a geographical-historical framework for their identity.

Simultaneously, adolescents strive to find a place in society that reconciles their self-perception with the recognition of their community. In other words, the shaping of children's inner identities as they imitate significant adults has an impact on society. As children learn from the constant back-and-forth relationship with the stimulus of their environment, it leads to an overall shift in perceptions and generational attitudes.

Play

Play is another significant experience that builds children's cognitive processes. At its most basic level, play allows students to act out imaginary realities, grasp their understanding of figures and objects in their environments, imitate prominent figures around them, and sift through behaviors, marking them "okay" and "not okay" accordingly. Play is not just some silly behavior that children seem to live for at every moment of their day; it is an inherent survival skill that helps them learn ways of being through practice. Furthermore, play is not just a child's practice; it is a continued need that extends in different forms into adulthood.

Education is a human extension of play.[33] This is evident in various games, including board, computer, role play, puzzle, scavenger hunt, and sports games. Vygotsky posed an exciting perspective on the importance of play for children when considering the nature of following imaginary play rules. All play inevitably involves rules for interacting with the environment and predetermined conditions the players must abide by. Introspectively, Vygotsky stated:

> The simplest game with rules immediately turns into an imaginary situation in the sense that as soon as the game is regulated by certain rules, a number of possibilities for action are ruled out. Every imaginary situation contains rules in a concealed form, [and] every game with rules contains an imaginary situation in a concealed form. The development from games with an overt imaginary situation and covert rules to games with overt rules and a covert imaginary situation outlines the evolution of children's play. . . . It is here that the child learns to act in a cognitive, rather than an externally visual realm by relying on internal tendencies and motives and not on incentives supplied by external things . . . in play things lose their determining force. The child sees one thing but acts differently in relation to what he sees. Thus a condition is reached in which the child begins to act independently of what he sees.[34]

In other words, play and its rules, and imagination allow children to practice living in other dispositions, in the reality of others. The rules that they did not necessarily experience before must be followed to socially interact in the game. This allows for a loosening of one's tethered senses by requiring the interplay of one's realities with that of others.

Implications of Learning and Nature versus Nurture

I. **Nature and Nurture Interplay:** The association between a child and their environment is complex, with both nature (genetics) and nurture (environmental influences) constantly interacting to shape learning and development.

II. **Sensory-Dependent Development:** Environmental stimuli and rich sensory input is needed to enhance neuronal connections and promote children's brain growth.

III. **Imitation and Social Influence:** Children learn by imitating the mannerisms, attentions, and responses of the significant persons in their lives.

IV. **Play as Learning:** Play is a vital aspect of a child's learning processes, allowing them to practice and understand the world around them by abiding by imaginary rules and viewing problems from different perspectives.

THE THREE PROMINENT LEARNING THEORIES USED IN SCHOOLS TODAY

For ages, parents and educators have dynamically speculated on how children learn. And after years of trying to figure that out, we have roughly a million answers. As you can imagine, regional differences, cultural variations, generational differences, technological advances, philosophies coming and going, psychological advancements . . . the list goes on and on, and these variables have led us down many paths. Some of these paths are helpful, and some are not, but judgment on learning approaches lies in what is best for our children.

However, among the immense nuances and adaptations in learning theories, three primary schools of thought have emerged and occupy spaces in present-day schools. These three theories are behaviorism, cognitivism, and constructivism. Having a better idea of what these theories entail can help both parents and teachers make informed academic choices for our children, including offering targeted support at home.

Behaviorism

Behaviorism is one of the earliest learning theories, yet since its emergence, it has probably garnered the most controversy. The premise of behaviorism is that kids learn through conditioned environments. They, and all persons for that matter, are in a constant state of reacting to actions that have been acted upon them. Therefore, children can be trained to behave in specific ways depending on the type of conditioning and the desired result.

A notable educator of this mindset was Edward L. Thorndike, who designed behaviorist learning principles during the first half of the twentieth century. Thorndike lectured that learning was the result of brain connections acquired through responding to stimuli. More specifically, Thorndike argued that learning results from trial and error.[35]

With animal observations, Thorndike concluded that humans, like animals, do things because they are motivated to do them. They learn to do something because the action that they are doing will bring them some reward like praise, a sense of belonging, or love. Therefore, kids will learn if part of the conditioning involves something they innately need or want.

Burrhus Frederic (B. F.) Skinner, another notable behaviorist, made his mark on learning theories by using operant conditioning experiments to test animals' propensity to react in specific ways to specific stimuli after a pattern of stimulus and consequences had been formed. These experiments helped Skinner to conclude that animals, perhaps like humans, could be conditioned to act in desired ways when an intentional stimulus was introduced into an environment and reinforced consistently.[36] He used rats in these animal experiments and observed their reactions to food stimuli in his infamous "Skinner Box."

IMPLICATIONS OF BEHAVIORISM

1. **Teacher-Centered Learning Environment:** A structured and teacher-directed approach to learning in the classroom.
2. **Clear Objectives and Expectations:** Objectives and instructional agendas are made clear to students, and there is a focus on goal-oriented learning.
3. **Pre- and Post-Tests:** Routine pre-tests and post-tests are common practices, as well as consistent feedback.
4. **Conditioning and Response Stimulation:** Conditioning is emphasized so that students can learn specific responses to specific stimuli. Experiences that would be considered distractions are minimized.
5. **Cue Usage:** There is a frequent use of cues to bring about desired responses. Parents can expect the use of cues and reinforcement to guide their child's learning.
6. **Reward Economy Systems:** Rewarding desired behavior and learning outcomes is very frequent.

7. **Environmental Modifications:** The environment is intentionally designed to encourage desired behaviors and discourage undesired behaviors; instructors often practice proactive approaches.
8. **Transparency:** Students are clearly informed of the learning objectives and daily tasks before they engage in them.

Cognitivism

Cognitivism developed as a method of scientifically understanding learning as a reasoning process. Additionally, it began to serve as a direct counter to behaviorist theories. Cognitivists scrutinized behaviorists for their views, claiming that their understanding of learning processes was overly simplified, and that cognition could not be explained by a call-and-response method.[37] Some notable educational psychologists, such as Jean Piaget, argued that human learning was much more complex and the brain was capable of reasoning and abstract thinking, which was not only a result of conditioning. Cognitivists view the brain as similar to a computer, essentially, that computes information as it is received to form memories, make connections, and make informed decisions regarding how to store and what to do with the information.

MULTIPLE INTELLIGENCES

The multiple intelligence theory principally falls under the cognitivist umbrella. Although many schools in North America prioritize only certain course subjects, such as math and language arts, Howard Gardner suggested that there are many other types of intelligence.[38] He distinguished nine types of intelligence that could be used to observe ways of knowing and their divergent differences.[39] Gardner proposed that the following were types of intelligence:

- Logical-mathematical
- Linguistic
- Visual-spatial
- Musical
- Naturalist
- Bodily-kinesthetic
- Interpersonal
- Intrapersonal
- Existential

Thus, in alignment with the multiple intelligence theory, intelligence can vary drastically among these categories, and there is no type of intelligence that is necessarily better than any other. Therefore, teaching can be done in multiple learning modalities and without the sense that some students are inherently "smarter" than others.

Furthermore, Gardner also contended that intelligence, and what was considered "a smartness," was culturally and socially dependent. Depending on the region that a child lives in, their intelligence and ability to process information is reliant upon the cultural values of that region. Along these lines, the implications for considering multiple intelligences in the classroom and the children's homes can have a significant impact not only on approaches to learning and teaching but also on cultivating strong self-concepts and growth mindsets among them.

Implications of Multiple Intelligences

1. **Diverse Instructional Approaches:** Offering a variety of teaching methods, such as discussions, debates, creative performances, and problem-solving, can help all students, regardless of their learning styles or intelligences, to excel in different ways.
2. **Multiple** Intelligences: Recognizing and catering to various forms of intelligence, such as verbal-linguistic, logical-mathematical, visual-spatial, and more, can empower students to leverage their unique strengths and abilities.
3. **Encouraging Self-Awareness:** It's important for students to understand their own intellectual strengths and weaknesses so that they can set intentional and personal learning goals.
4. **Holistic Learning:** The goal of education is to nurture students' growth as well-rounded learners who can apply their intelligence in various contexts.

Culturally Responsive Learning

Culturally responsive teaching is another extension of cognitivism. Its premise is that learning is conditional upon one making connections to preexisting neuronal relationships. Therefore, when learning is culturally relevant, it is more of a natural cognitive process in which the child learns new information productively and independently. Neurons are more apt to make new connections when there already exists some resemblance to what is presented to them.

Additionally, learning can become engaging, with sensory input aligned with established motivators. Cultural ways of knowing become hard-wired as children are consistently exposed to specific environmental stimuli and mimic what influential individuals do in their communities.[40]

Culture is any agreed upon set of ways of being. Therefore, examples of culture would include special interest groups, sports, food, clothing, music, language, and visual arts. Thus, in the educational sense, engagement and retention of knowledge are enhanced as learners draw upon sensory inputs that resemble norms from their cultural contexts.

Implications of Cognitivism

1. **Active and Meaningful Learning:** Cognitivism emphasizes that learning is an active and meaningful process that requires students to engage as critical thinkers, drawing upon preexisting connections.
2. **Importance of Background and Context:** The student's background, the learning environment, and adult support are central factors in cognitive learning.
3. **Inner Dialogue and Self-Regulation:** Introspective and reflective strategies are beneficial, fostering, inner dialogue, self-regulation, and other metacognitive habits.
4. **Culturally Responsive Instruction:** Instruction should incorporate approaches that are culturally relevant to activate prior knowledge and enhance neuronal connections and productive memory formation.
5. **Multiple Intelligences:** Students have a variety of intelligences, and instructional approaches that consider intellectual variations can have significant motivational effects on learners and promote diverse types of knowledge.
6. **Sensory Engagement:** Instruction should include sensory triggers and visualizations to help information move through working memory effectively.
7. **Goal Setting and Organization:** The use of advanced graphic organizers and goal-setting strategies can help students organize information and develop cognitive skills.

Constructivism

The third foundational learning theory is constructivism. Constructivists are concerned with learning that occurs through socially relevant experiences and collaboration. The premise is that learning should be a constructed process in which meaningful tasks are completed using real-world contexts. Constructivists understand learning as an extraordinarily unique process that does not depend on hard facts or universal truths when considering value systems connected to types of knowledge. Knowledge is regarded as a construction of one's reality and what one finds essential to solving problems directly related to them.[41]

Therefore, constructivist learning cannot be a passive process. It is instead a dynamic and actionable process where the instructor facilitates what the learner needs and is careful not to force their own knowledge upon them.[42] Additionally, learning does not have to occur within the traditional four-walled classroom. Learning in various environments, especially those directly related to the content of study, is encouraged.[43] Therefore, spaces such as sports fields, labs, school hallways, museums, and gardens, to name a few, are desirable learning environments. Furthermore, within these environmental contexts, hands-on activities, collaborative group projects, and community advocacy are emphasized.

Constructivist approaches, during their immersive introduction to society, were innovative at the time. Thus, constructivists became known as progressive educators and were considered part of the progressive education movement. Many well-known educators and influencers were a part of this movement. Booker T. Washington, John Dewey, and Lev Vygotsky were among the most notable.

CRITICAL THEORY AND CRITICAL PEDAGOGY

Critical pedagogy is an extension of both critical theory and constructivism. This approach to learning focuses on the marginalization of subpopulations, with learning approaches that support the identification of the roots of such marginalization and problem-solving skills that can subvert marginalizing practices. In other words, critical pedagogy is based on an educational philosophy that places a strong emphasis on understanding and confronting the systemic factors that lead to the exclusion or disadvantage of specific subpopulations.

This learning approach encourages students to critically examine and question the underlying causes of such inequalities through a combination of project and inquiry-based tasks. Furthermore, these tasks are typically geared toward identifying solutions that seek to change oppressive practices. In essence, critical pedagogy empowers students to become active agents in transforming their own educational experiences as well as their environments outside of the school.

In this way, the learning connects to the personalized and experiential neuronal connections of students to instill critical hope, independent thinking, and meaningful learning that liberates them in various ways.[44] This can be useful to parents and teachers when advocacy for critical thinking and social equity are prioritized components of the academic experience. Additionally, critical pedagogy can aid students in preparing to navigate a wide range of diverse social environments and situations.

Implications of Constructivism

1. **Social Interaction and Communication:** Communication and social interaction are central in a constructivist classroom, fostering shared social constructs.
2. **Teacher Facilitation and Encouragement:** Constructivist teachers facilitate complex group conversations and support individual student problem-solving with meaningful and hands-on learning experiences.
3. **Creativity and Critical Thinking:** Constructivist educators promote creativity and critical thinking by asking questions and engaging in tasks that encourage higher-order thinking skills.
4. **Active Learning Strategies:** The constructivist approach involves taking students on trips, group work, investigation/discovery, hands-on projects, and flexible curriculum negotiation.
5. **Student Responsibility:** Constructivism emphasizes students being actively directive and accountable for their learning.

SUMMARY

The historical question of whose knowledge is most valuable and how it should be transposed to children has long been a point of interest and contention. Various historical approaches to education, from ancient Egyptian and precolonial models to Confucian, Socratic, Platonic, and Aristotelian philosophies, were examined to illuminate how learning and teaching models have evolved. Strategizing what students should know and how they can most effectively come to know connects these various philosophies. These connections are evident today in our understanding of how people learn and how we approach teaching.

Additionally, understanding the interplay between nature (genetics) and nurture (environmental influences) is crucial to comprehending and shaping children's learning and development. Nature and nurture work in a see-saw relationship, thriving in sensory-rich environments and working together to enhance neuronal connections. Imitation, social influence, and play are essential components of nature-nurture collaboration.

Lastly, teaching approaches have diverged under the principles of three main learning theories: behaviorism, cognitivism, and constructivism. Practices such as the teacher-centered learning environment, clear objectives, pre- and post-tests, conditioning, cue usage, reward economy systems, environmental modifications, and transparency have emerged in educational settings from what we know about how children learn. For each model, implications and various insights for parents and educators promote children's overall growth and development. These insights, implications, and concrete applications will be the focus of part III.

NOTES

1. Judith Jurgens, "The Teaching of Khety Twice—A New Reading of oBM EA 65597 as a School Exercise," *The Journal of Egyptian Archaeology* 105, 1 (2020): 127–34.
2. Tahmer Fahim and Nagoua Zoair, "Education in Ancient Egypt till the End of the Graeco-Roman Period: Some Evidences for Quality," *Journal of Association of Arab Universities for Tourism and Hospitality* 13, 3 (2016): 1–16.
3. Adolf Erman, *The Literature of the ancient Egyptians: Poems, Narratives, and Manual of Instruction from the Third and Second Millennia B.C.*, translated by Aylward M. Blackman (London: Routledge Revivals, 1927), 299.
4. Fahim and Zoair, "Education in Ancient Egypt," 1–16.
5. Jurgens, "The Teaching of Khety Twice," 127–34.
6. Fahim and Zoair, "Education in Ancient Egypt," 1–16.
7. Fahim and Zoair, "Education in Ancient Egypt," 1–16.
8. Silvance Abeka, *Introduction to Higher Education* (Simple Book Publishing, n.d.).
9. Abeka, *Introduction to Higher Education*.
10. Abeka, *Introduction to Higher Education*.
11. Gerald Gutek, *Historical and Philosophical Foundations of Education: A Biographical Introduction* (New York: Pearson, 2011).
12. Gutek, *Historical and Philosophical Foundations of Education*.
13. Confucius, *The Analects of Confucius: A Philosophical Translation*, translated by Roger T. Ames and Henry Rosemont Jr. (New York: Ballantine Books, 1999).
14. Gutek, *Historical and Philosophical Foundations of Education*.
15. Ying-Chih Chen, "Epistemic Uncertainty and the Support of Productive Struggle During Scientific Modeling for Knowledge Co-development," *Journal of Research in Science Teaching* 59, 3 (2022): 383–422.
16. Gutek, *Historical and Philosophical Foundations of Education*.
17. Aristotle, *The Basic Works of Aristotle*, edited by R. McKeon (New York: Modern Library, 2001).
18. Aristotle, *The Basic Works of Aristotle*.
19. Bruce E. Wexler, *Brain and Culture: Neurobiology, Ideology, and Social Change* (Cambridge, MA: The MIT Press, 2008), 38.
20. MIT Technology Review, *New Measures of Human Brain Processing Speed*, August 25, 2009, https://www.technologyreview.com/2009/08/25/210267/new-measure-of-human-brain-processing-speed/.

21. Wexler, *Brain and Culture*.
22. Wexler, *Brain and Culture*.
23. Zaretta Hammond, *Culturally Responsive Teaching and the Brain: Promoting Authentic Engagement and Rigor among Culturally and Linguistically Diverse Students* (New York: Corwin Press, 2015), 49.
24. Wexler, *Brain and Culture*, 30.
25. Wexler, *Brain and Culture*.
26. Wexler, *Brain and Culture*.
27. Wexler, *Brain and Culture*, 101.
28. Jean Piaget, *Play, Dreams, and Imitation in Childhood* (New York: Norton & Co., 1962).
29. Wexler, *Brain and Culture*.
30. Roberta G. Simmons and Dale A. Blythe, *Moving into Adolescence: The Impact of Pubertal Change and School Context* (New York: Routledge, 1987).
31. Wexler, *Brain and Culture*.
32. Erik Erikson, "The Problem of Ego Identity," in *Pivotal Papers on Identification*, edited by G.H. Pollock (Madison, CT: International Universities Press, 1959).
33. Wexler, *Brain and Culture*.
34. Lev Vygotsky, "The Role of Play in Development," in *Mind in Society*, translated by M. Cole (Cambridge, MA: Harvard University Press, 1978), 92–104.
35. Dale Schunk, *Learning Theories: An Educational Perspective* (New York: Pearson, 2012).
36. B.F. Skinner, "Whatever Happened to Psychology as the Science of Behavior?" *American Psychologist* 42, 8 (1987): 784.
37. Edward Tolman, "Instinct and Purpose," *Psychological Review* 27, 3 (1920): 217–33.
38. Howard Gardner, *Multiple Intelligences* (New York: Basic Books, 1993).
39. Howard Gardner, *Frames of Mind: The Theory of Multiple Intelligences* (New York: Basic Books, 1983).
40. Hammond, *Culturally Responsive Teaching and the Brain*.
41. Schunk, *Learning Theories*.
42. Donald Generals, Jr., "The Architect of Progressive Education: John Dewey or Booker T. Washington," *National Association of African American Studies & National Association of Hispanic and Latino Studies: 2000 Literature Monograph Series. Proceedings (Education Section) (Houston, TX, February 21–26, 2000)* (2002): 186.
43. Booker T. Washington, "Principal's Annual Report," unpublished manuscript, Tuskegee Institute, BTW Papers, Library of Congress, 1902.
44. Jeffrey M. R. Duncan-Andrade, "Note to Educators: Hope Required When Growing Roses in Concrete," *Harvard Educational Review* 79, 2 (2009): 181–94.

Part III

Implications and Applications

The last two decades have seen expansive developments in brain research. Coupled with our foundational knowledge of learning theory, these developments will have tremendous influence on how we educate our children both in our homes and in American classrooms. In a seminal research study sponsored by the National Research Council, we learned:

> Pedagogical content knowledge is different from knowledge of general teaching methods. Expert teachers know the structure of their disciplines, and this knowledge provides them with cognitive roadmaps that guide the assignments they give students, the assessments the use to gauge students' progress, and the questions they ask in the give and take of classroom life. In short, their knowledge of the discipline and their knowledge of pedagogy interact. But knowledge of the discipline structure does not in itself guide the teacher.[1]

After an analysis of how the brain learns, part I concluded by providing some general implications for teachers and parents. Part II provided a similar approach to describing implications after a description of contemporary teaching and learning theories. This section will now delve into more granular detail in describing the brain and learning theory–compatible *implications* for teachers and parents, alike. For their part, teachers can re-examine their approach to curriculum development, their pedagogy, the types of assignments they give, and how they assess both their students' learning and the effectiveness of their own teaching.

Parents can discern ways they can support the efforts of their children's teachers and become more effective in preparing their sons and daughters in the formative preschool years as well as times away from school. The last portion of part III is devoted to *applications*—examples teachers and parents can use to recreate their own versions of lessons, assignments, and assessments.

The emerging implications are clear and specific. Much of what has been learned can be applied immediately to classrooms and homes, and much of it supports the good teaching many educators and parents are already doing. At the same time, these implications might also challenge some of what has been believed to be good teaching and should require some deep introspection and soul-searching. In describing the more authentic and natural learning environment of the future, Dr. Robert Sylwester shares:

> [Biologist Gerald] Edelman's model of our brain . . . a junglelike brain might thrive best in a junglelike classroom that includes many sensory, cultural, and problem layers that are closely related to the real-world environment . . . that best stimulates the neural networks. . . . It's interesting to muse on such widely acclaimed developments as thematic curricula, cooperative learning, and portfolio assessment. All require more effort from teachers than do traditional forms of curriculum, instruction, and evaluation.[2]

Moreover, we can learn a great deal from the various learning theories—all of which have specific direct application to our classrooms and our home environments.[3] Part III will bring this brain research and learning theory[4] together for a cogent and robust model of teaching and learning, where students actively construct their own learning rather than passively receive it as static sponges.

Just as we expect students to practice metacognition, or thinking about how they think, we must expect reflection of our own learning and of our own teaching. Knowing how we ourselves learn will help us appreciate how to connect our children to the content, but we must also acknowledge that not all our students will approach learning the same way we do. In so doing, not only will we better grasp the process of learning, but we will model the requisite skills of metacognition for our aspiring learners.

Sadly, our conventional class structures and teaching models are often inflexible and may not lend themselves to multiple teaching approaches or learning styles. This can then lead to a poorer quality of student learning. In the words of Jane Healy, "[i]t never occurred to us that the rigid system of which we were a part might be contributing to the problem."[5] One size—one approach—does not fit all students, or even all learning outcomes. More succinctly, different learning outcomes often need different teaching strategies.

Further, many of our teaching preferences have been influenced by cultural norms. For instance, in North America, the traditional educational approaches have been largely influenced by the industrial revolution, and international competitiveness through a Eurocentric lens. Consequently, many conventional approaches to teaching have involved cramming students with content for their memorization and immediate recitation on standardized exams—lower levels on Bloom's Taxonomy. As such, many approaches focus on an individualist ethos compared to more collectivist norms as espoused by other cultures.

With a bit of reconsideration, and the support of brain research and learning theory, educators can make modest changes to their classroom instruction and perhaps have profound impact on their students. The same holds true for parents—perhaps we can be more purposeful in providing authentic learning opportunities for our children. The implications and subsequent applications to follow range from the classroom environment to lesson design, from pedagogy to assignments, and from the assessment of students learning to that of our own teaching.

IMPLICATIONS

The Learning Environment

Once our brains feel safe to explore and try new things, they seek relevance to the information before them. Our brains then thrive on and seek challenging and novel material and learning opportunities. This is how people are motivated, and therefore such cognitive opportunities use multiple regions of the brain to make stronger and lasting connections which can be drawn upon for future learning. Ken Bain explains how the best educators view their students:

> Highly effective teachers tend to reflect a strong trust in students. They usually believe that students want to learn, and they assume, until proven otherwise, that they can. They often display openness with students and may, from time to time, talk about their own intellectual journey, its ambitions, triumphs, frustrations, and failures, and encourage their students to be similarly reflective and candid. . . . Above all, they tend to treat students with what can only be called simple decency.[6]

What Bain is really suggesting is a teaching mindset of student assets as opposed to student deficits. Orthodox ideology would suggest students come to the classroom with deficits or gaps in their learning, and it is the job of the teacher to fill in those gaps. Rather, asset thinking focuses on the assets, the prior knowledge and experiences students bring to the classroom. Such a shift in ideology can have a profound impact on curriculum design and pedagogy. Parents should leverage the notion that children bring a zest to learn and seek ways to connect and expand on the knowledge, skills, and dispositions they already possess. Learning is natural and connecting; it is not sterile and isolating.

The classroom can be an emotional place for students. In fact, teachers should carefully capitalize on emotional connections to their content. Robert Sylwester emphasizes, "[w]e know emotion is very important to the educative process because it drives attention, which drives learning and memory."[7] Laurie Materna elaborates: "Stronger emotions promote greater recall, while engaging too few emotions in the learning process tends to cause learners to quickly forget material unless it is rehearsed repeatedly."[8] Energy, feelings, and wonderment bring the learning environment to life and make new knowledge stick.

We have learned the human brain plays a central role in motivation. The brain is naturally motivated by a sense of curiosity, anticipation, and relevance.[9] Parents and teachers should take advantage of children's inherent tendency to want to find answers, to predict next steps, and for their search for meaning in what they do. They want to take ownership for their own learning, and they need to be given the opportunity—the dignity—to take ownership for their own struggle.[10] As such, the astute educator helps the student find why the topic is relevant to them. Jane Healy identified three general principles of learner motivation: "[I]n order for any of us to be motivated for a particular task, three ingredients must be present: emotional connection, challenge, and payoff. The most effective payoff, however, takes the form of internal (intrinsic) satisfaction rather than external (extrinsic) reward."[11] The National Academies of Sciences, Engineering, and Medicine explains, in part: "When learners believe they have control over their learning environment, they are more likely to take on challenges and persist with difficult tasks. Evidence suggests that the opportunity to make meaningful choices during instruction, even if they are small, can support autonomy, motivation, and ultimately, learning and achievement."[12]

The implications are critical for instructors. Before learning can take place, the students must feel safe and able to take cognitive risks. If their brains sense danger—or embarrassment, for example—their priority will not be on learning. One of the primary ways to help students to become motivated is to guide them to take their own control, to be self-motivated, and to create their own challenges. Payoff comes in the form of knowing they can succeed at the challenges they set for themselves for something they find intrinsically rewarding; they develop a sense of self-efficacy.

Such approaches are critical if we are to meet the foundational levels of Maslow's Hierarchy of Needs. These first two critical levels show that if students are to learn, they must have their physiological and safety and security needs met. Likewise, the students' feelings of belonging and being needed or valued are important considerations for teachers. The classroom environment plays a central role in preparing the conditions for student learning, as such.

We further know the human brain is a social brain. Not only do students yearn for social connection, they look for opportunities to contribute to others. Bransford and his colleagues explained: "Learners . . . are motivated when they see the usefulness of what they are learning and when they can use that information to do something that has an impact on others—especially their local community."[13] This insight again supports the hierarchical needs of student motivation explained by Maslow.

Jensen and McConchie provide a list of important long-term motivational strategies: "Autonomy, Student Empowerment, Success, Belonging, Social Status, and Challenge."[14] These contemporary notions support the attainment of the middle and upper levels of Maslow's original Needs Hierarchy for Motivation (figure 3.1).[15]

All of us, students and adults alike, are motivated in ascending order by our most basic physiological needs, the need for safety and security, a need for social belonging and love, self-esteem, and ultimately self-actualization. Even Maslow's later unpublished work proves to be prescient as he added cognitive, aesthetic, and finally transcendent needs—the penultimate level (figure 3.2).

It's obvious that if a student is urgently hungry or thirsty, their minds will wander and won't be focused on the learning tasks at hand. Likewise, if they should feel bullied or harassed, their attention will drift. Similarly, when a student doesn't feel appreciated by the instructor or classmates, they will feel isolated and will be less able to attend to instruction. Should they feel disempowered, not feel up to the task cognitively, nor feel they have little ability to meet the challenges ahead, they'll not likely be able to learn at an optimal level let alone to reach a state of self-actualization or even a sense of transcendence.

Our children need to have their most basic needs met. They need to feel safe and to belong socially, and to have a sense of self-efficacy. They need to feel they are making a difference. Keen educators will not only appreciate and embody these attributes, but they will deliberately set the tone in their classrooms and monitor for signs of concern from their students. These best teachers will provide opportunities for students to work together, to take on ownership and responsibility for their own learning and strive for an optimal level of challenge in their classrooms reaching into the community and connecting with the home.

Adults can help students take ownership of their own learning by teaching and modeling self-regulatory behavior. Students should set goals, plan ways to achieve them, and assess their progress.[16] As such, the students direct their own cognition and adjust as they learn. They practice metacognition. Teachers and parents can be supportive by accommodating student interests at appropriate cognitive levels.[17]

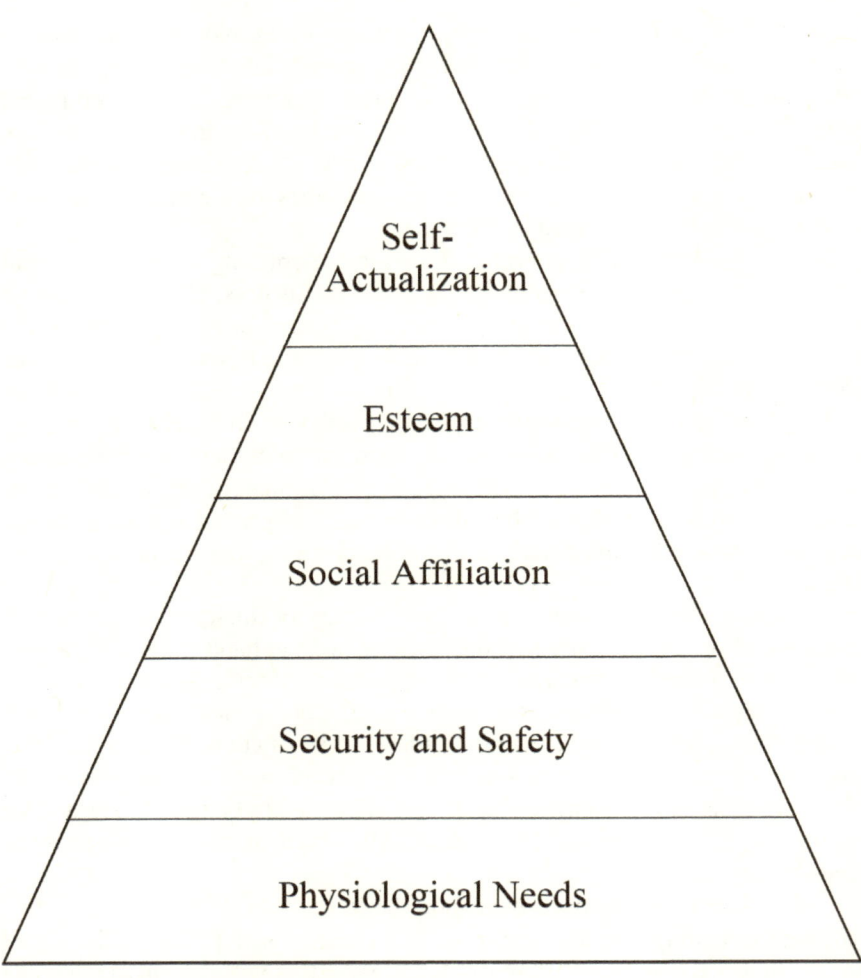

Figure 3.1 Maslow's Needs Hierarchy

To relate this to the science of learning—in terms of how the brain processes—all the sensory information that our brain receives from the outside world, with the exception of smell, enters the brain first through the brain stem where the information is screened to determine if danger exists and whether a fight or flight response is warranted. If it is determined that the environment is safe, the brain continues to process the incoming information up through the middle brain's limbic system where emotions get triggered and where preceding memories are scanned for both relevance and again for safety. All of this happens instantly, and higher-order thinking has not even yet occurred.

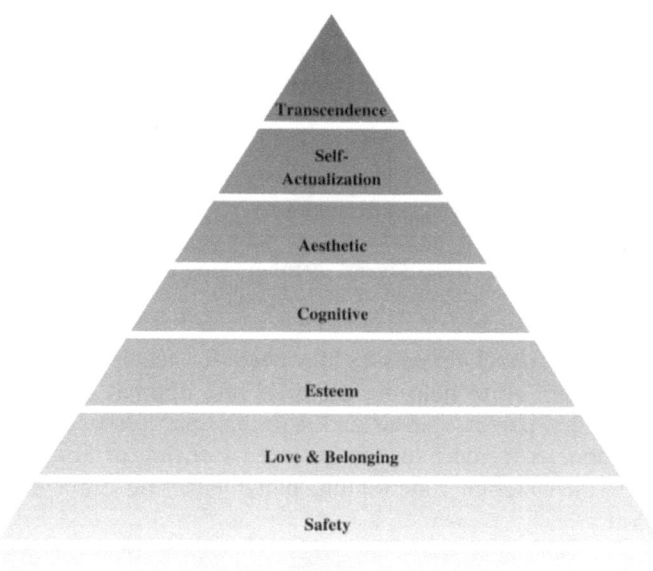

Figure 3.2 Maslow's Hierarchy of Needs with Transcendence

Our best teachers understand this and are certain to ensure their classrooms are a safe environment for learning to occur—a place for intellectual engagement and thinking to take place without a high level of stress.[18] These same teachers understand the critical importance of emotional relevance to each student's learning experience and therefore create an environment where students feel comfortable yet sufficiently challenged to engage with and to explore the content at hand, always looking for ways to connect to other experiences as well as to their future ambitions. Their brains seek novelty and challenge. Home can be a place for self-discovery and not a place or time for forced learning.

The behaviorist instructor would adapt the classroom environment to support positive stimuli and negate distractions and seek to activate prior knowledge. The constructivist instructor would create a classroom of appropriate high challenge but low risk—one that encourages creativity and critical thinking through social interaction. The classroom environment sets the tone for teaching and learning—for the curriculum and for pedagogy.

The arts and physical education are critical to brain development. At home, parents should provide opportunities for their children to explore their world and to take the lead in their own exploration. Song, dance, physical activity, and artistic experimentation are critical to the young child's mind. These same types of learning are surely just as critical once the child enters the school building. The arts and physical education need to then become infused into the curriculum as they help our youth to gain confidence and to integrate new learning into their memories, according to research.[19] Healy elaborated:

> Studies show that four-, five, and six-year-olds in heavily "academic" classes tend to become less creative and more anxious.... Youngsters in well-structured "play"-oriented preschools and developmentally appropriate primary grades develop more positive attitudes toward learning along with better ultimate skill development.[20]

Together, this research expresses the need for teachers and parents to work with one another to help our children find optimal success. Working with their teachers, parents can extend learning opportunities at home, both during the school year and over the summer. Infusion of arts and physical activity strengthen mental functioning, better ensuring brain development and cognition.

Curriculum and Pedagogy

Once our classroom environment is prepared as an emotionally safe space filled with relevant experiences for challenging learning to take place, we can focus on cognition. In part I, we learned how the brain develops, functions, and learns. While different regions of the brain play primary roles for different aspects of learning and memory, they all work together wholistically to function as the learning brain.[21] So, while there is some validity to left-brain and right-brain learners, some of these earlier suppositions were simply overstated. The whole brain works together and cannot function optimally in an isolated fashion.

Memories can be strengthened in the brain by using multiple approaches—kinesthetic, auditory, and visual, for example. In this way, different regions of the brain are engaged, and existing neurons are strengthened when students commit something to memory by writing, speaking, and listening. Memories created through multiple approaches are easier to recall when needed in the future. Repetition and continued practice further encourage neural growth,[22] and of course experiences situated in an emotional context are more likely to drive the learning home. Our homes are natural places for experiential learning opportunities.

Knowledge of how our brains learn has obvious implications for how we structure our classrooms, how we design our curriculum, and how we implement our pedagogy. For example, we need to create a pleasant classroom setting which encourages dynamic engagement with the content and social interaction along with opportunities to engage our varied senses. Importantly, the brain thinks in terms of visual imagery and not in text as in our largely text-dependent curriculum.

Suzanne Wade and her colleagues discovered that college students were more interested and retained textbook information better when the information was important, new, and valued; the information was unexpected; the text supported readers in making connections with prior knowledge or experience; the text contained imagery and descriptive language; and the author attempted to relate information to readers' background knowledge using, for example, comparisons and analogies.[23] Certainly, these implications hold true for K–12 students, as well.

Teachers can also use interactive mini lectures where they introduce a topic and students discuss how it can be applied in real-life settings or with their own experiences. These discussions can take place in small group settings. Leamnson expressed, "Properly done, there are few more effective devices for learning than studying in small groups . . . and study followed by individual reports would seem to provide optimal results."[24]

We all experience times when we are reading or listening to someone, and our minds begin to wander. We should take this as a signal to either consciously focus hard for a few more minutes, to take a break, or to switch up tasks for a few moments. Richard Restak quotes golf coach Jim McLean: "Practice only as long as you can concentrate. Stop when you . . . lose focus. Short, focused practice sessions are often the most productive."[25]

If we keep lecturing beyond the students' attention span, we're wasting our breath, and we're wasting learning opportunities. We simply need to switch up what we're doing in order to be more effective and productive. Sometimes we simply need to build in brain breaks for our students—breaks for only a couple of minutes.

Not all researchers will agree on the best way to reach learners, but they do agree on the necessity of using multiple approaches and through multiple senses. Colin Rose, for example stated that "learners remember 90 percent of what they see, hear, say, and do, as compared to only 20 percent of what they read, 30 percent of what they hear, 40 percent of what they see, 50 percent of what they say, and 60 percent of what they do."[26] The message is clear: use multiple instructional strategies and sensory modes where you can in order to afford your students the best opportunity to learn.

For optimal intellectual engagement, it is better to have our students become "note-makers" rather than "note-takers." Rather than passively taking notes, they need to engage and make sense of the material by creating notes in their own words. It is also beneficial for them to verbalize or discuss their notes that they make which not only helps them to clarify their thinking, but it also provides additional synaptic connections in the brain. As such, students will need help from their teachers as how to "make" notes—how to take what they hear and read, and then put into their own words and connect to their own experiences and context—to truly engage with the notes they are creating.

"The most effective teaching will be done by teachers who vary their approach, use different methods of instructing within the same class period, and never let their students get comfortable," according to Robert Leamnson.[27] This can be a matter of mixing mini lectures with discussion (small and large group), debate, visual aids, hands-on activity, writing, problem-solving—all with the intent to emotionally connect, to find relevance and meaning, and to connect to the material. Such multiple approaches not only help to keep the students' attention, but they also use multiple parts of their brains and are more likely to incorporate learning across various regions of the brain in a more dynamic fashion.

In an interesting study, researchers found that typing notes is less impactful on student writing than when students hand-write notes and put the notes in their own words.[28] The former is a more passive approach and doesn't necessarily invite cognitive engagement, while the latter is more assertive in nature, requiring student intellectual engagement.

One common element to all this previous discussion is that of time. It takes time to learn, and it takes time to teach. Students need to be given time to intellectually grapple with the content they are being taught. Time is needed for them to think, to write, to discuss, to practice in project form. Educators not only need to use time strategically in their instruction and their assignments, but also in how they ask questions. They purposefully use wait-time.

There are two forms of wait-time. The first wait-time occurs when the teacher asks the class a question. After they ask a question, they typically call on a single student for a response. The average amount of this wait-time is an astonishing 1.5 seconds, at most. The student called upon has little time to reflect, to think, and to provide an answer.

Furthermore, all the other students are relieved not to have to provide an answer and can stop thinking. Instructors should experiment with their own wait-time and give students more time to think. Likewise, they should consider strategies where all students need to respond, not just the one. For example, all students could be asked to write a response or to share with others. The idea is to get all students sufficient time to be challenged to think and to engage with the concepts.

The second wait-time occurs after the student has provided their answer. All teachers are prone to feel compelled to respond immediately. We acknowledge their answer with affirmation, negation, or some other nuanced retort. But the student is typically off the hook at this point. If we wait—if we don't respond immediately to their answer, the student will be searching inside to determine whether they were correct. They may choose to elaborate. In other words, they will be thinking. These two wait-times intuitively make a great deal of sense to excellent teachers. But the challenge to effectively implement them is more difficult than it might appear. Parents have tremendous opportunity to practice this second wait-time at home.

Once we have a firm understanding of the basic principles of how the brain learns, educators can re-examine their curriculum to determine how best to teach their content. Writing for the National Research Council, John Bransford and his colleagues stipulated:

The fact that experts' knowledge is organized around important ideas or concepts suggests that curricula should also be organized in ways that lead to conceptual understanding. Many approaches to curriculum design make it difficult for students to organize knowledge meaningfully. Often there is only superficial coverage of facts before moving on to the next topic; there is little time to develop important, organizing ideas.[29]

A recurring theme in this book is that students create their own learning by active engagement, making personally meaningful relevance of the content, and practicing metacognition of their own learning. This is considered a learner-centered classroom.[30] However, students may have erroneous prior content knowledge or conceptual knowledge, or they may not have the intellectual tools required to navigate new material. Our feedback, therefore, needs to be specific and targeted,[31] and it needs to be developmentally appropriate.

Hence, an intersection of a learner-centered approach with a knowledge-centered approach is necessary. Again, Bransford and his colleagues express: "Knowledge-centered environments also focus on the kinds of information and activities that help students develop an understanding of disciplines."[32] The best instructors walk the fine line of focusing on both the content and the knowledge, and on how to best reach individual student's learning.

Too often the conventional curriculum is structured in isolation from other content and other disciplines. This is most often a concern in middle and high school. Such an isolated approach makes it virtually impossible for students to see and understand the bigger unified whole, one that promotes integration for new meaning and understanding. Memorizing facts or concepts in isolation from context does not promote optimal learning. Such traditional approaches are teacher-based models of instruction. But more contemporary learning theories provide insights to mitigate these concerns. According to Bransford and his colleagues:

An alternative . . . is to expose students to the major features of a subject domain as they arise naturally in problem situations. Activities can be structured so that students are able to explore, explain, extend, and evaluate their progress. Ideas are best introduced when students see a need or a reason for their use—this helps them see relevant uses of knowledge to make sense of what they are learning.[33]

Moreover, our traditional approaches to teaching and learning have provided a singular, often erroneous, perspective of how we identify giftedness, often through such measures as IQ and standardized tests. Michio Kaku was clear: IQ tests "actually give no definition of intelligence in the first place."[34] Such ways of identifying our best students frequently keep us from identifying creative and otherwise truly gifted and talented students. English language learner student intelligence is often missed entirely with such examinations.

According to Jane Healy, these other prodigious students prefer to use more strategic than problem-solving approaches, seek patterns and relationships, connect concepts in knowledge webs, prefer complexity, are adventurous in their learning, and are self-disciplined in their academic pursuits.[35] These are the sorts of learning experiences that help all students, irrespective if they have been deemed as gifted, make sense of the content.

Finally, Healy implores teachers to be purposeful in their curriculum design and pedagogy. She asks that students be given opportunities to work together, and for self-evaluation to be routinely practiced. In particular, "A creative classroom is not an excuse for mayhem or disorganization. Master teachers who focus on creative enrichments carefully plan and evaluate each activity."[36]

According to Bransford and his colleagues:

> An alternative ... is to expose students to the major features of a subject domain as they arise naturally in problem situations. Activities can be structured so that students are able to explore, explain, extend, and evaluate their progress. Ideas are best introduced when students see a need or a reason for their use—this helps them see relevant uses of knowledge to make sense of what they are learning.[37]

As teachers begin their pedagogical job of engaging their students with the content, they need to be comfortable with their role not as a "sage on the stage," but more the "guide on the side," or an expert who helps students wrestle with the content, to scaffold off previous learning, and to connect with authentic and meaningful experiences. Such teaching and learning are not purely linear and concrete; it is dynamic, organic, and malleable, just like the human brain. Stephen Covey said some of his best lessons lived on the edge of chaos.[38] As such, these contemporary classrooms move from one dominated by teacher-centered instruction, to learner-centered or even learning-centered instruction.

We also need to reconsider the role and utility of conventional lectures. Lectures are good vehicles to get across material, especially factual, in a relatively short period of time. The model is based, however, on the belief that knowledge can be transmitted to and subsequently absorbed by the students. It's a passive approach to learning. Still, lectures can show students not only what content the teacher believes to be most important to learn, but also lecturers can show students what and how experts think.

Higher-order thinking and understanding of the material cannot be conveyed in the conventional manner,[39] however. Robert Leamnson suggests some alternative techniques to traditional lectures:

Dialogue with Students. Take the time each lesson to focus on dialogue with just a few students to monitor their understanding and progress, and to help them think deeply about new concepts.

The Interrupted Lecture. Shorter, or mini, lectures are more effective than one prolonged lecture. A break between lectures provides students the opportunity to recalibrate and to intellectually integrate what they've learned, perhaps through discussion or other activity.

Progress Report on an Assignment. Students can benefit immensely from one-on-one interaction with a professor before or after class to dive deep into a topic. This provides the students the opportunity to think deeply and engage in ways they might not otherwise, but it also provides the professor the opportunity to learn what the students know, as well as where their understanding is faulty.

Give Students a Chance to Instruct. When students are expected to teach their peers, they are forced to really study a topic—to understand it to a degree they might not otherwise as a passive recipient of a lecture. Such practices take time, of course, and the professor must monitor for accuracy and clarity.

Debate the Debatable. Giving students the opportunity to formulate a logical argument, to present their case, and in turn to listen to counterarguments has immense benefits. Like the previous techniques, this strategy requires active engagement and oversight by the professor, and it of course takes more time than a straightforward lecture.[40]

By stretching the learners' intellectual rubber bands, the teacher can create cognitive dissonance. For instance, if a youth believes X, but their actions are aligned with Y, there will be an obvious cognitive disconnect, and they will naturally want to rid themselves of this angst. They may change their action or perhaps their belief from such an intellectual struggle. After all, adults do not want to be passive sponges; they desire the freedom of ownership and responsibility in their own learning and thinking. The classroom is an optimal place to explore, to challenge, and to be challenged.

Pulling the finer points of learning theory together, we know that learning is contextual and is most successful when prior learning is activated and used to scaffold new concepts. As such, teachers need to work from students' existing knowledge and bring in long-term memory to help lay the foundation for new learning. It is helpful for students to use multiple senses when they approach new concepts and to find the content relevant to their lives. Parents can create opportunities for additional experiences outside the classroom—to provide additional contexts and extend the experiences of the classroom.

Assignments

Assignments need to flow directly from the content objectives and extend from the corresponding instruction. In other words, educators begin with the end in mind—the goals and objectives for the unit. They then design lessons and instruction to reach those goals and objectives. The assignments should be natural extensions of this instruction. Since so much learning takes place outside the classroom, teachers need to take advantage of this time through their assignments to make them relevant and productive. Parents can play a critical role here.

For the most part, there should be less reliance on simplistic traditional worksheets, with the exception of lab sheets or study guides, for example. Again, Bloom's Taxonomy would serve as a perfect model to help the instructor gear assignments to varying levels of higher-order thinking, always based on the goals and objectives of the content, of course. Opportunities for analysis, synthesis, evaluation, and creation should be considered. This is where the real dynamic learning takes place.

This suggests that more authentic and reality-based assignments are optimal. Such assignments can be problem-based or community-based, but they need to be relevant to the students' lives, and the students need to see the relevance. In its 2018 report on *How People Learn II*, the National Academies of Science, Engineering, and Medicine noted, in part:

> A number of studies suggest that situational interest can be a strong predictor of engagement, positive attitudes, and performance, including a study of students' essay writing[41] and other research.[42] These studies suggest the power of situational interest for engaging students in learning, which has implications for the design of project-based or problem-based learning.[43]

Problem- or project-based assignments focus on process as opposed to learning outcomes. According to Barbara Condliffe and her colleagues, "The challenge should be one that drives students to grapple with central concepts and principles of a discipline and to develop constructive investigations that resemble projects adults might do outside of school."[44] Developmental portfolios are prime repositories of authentic assignments that can most certainly be relevant and problem-based. Such developmental portfolios can exist within a course or even extend across a student's entire academic program.

Anyone who has served as an employer and hired workers understands the necessity of authentic experiences when looking for new employees. The conventional high school transcript does not tell an employer much. In fact, employers don't use transcripts at the point of hire. They only use the transcripts for credential verification—a human resources function. Frankly, the traditional transcript does not tell an employer anything too important. All students today take virtually the same courses and earn roughly the same grades. Transcripts don't serve the purpose of differentiating candidates. What sets the best potential employees apart from the rest?

Portfolios of authentic, real-life experiences can make the difference. Portfolios are tangible examples of work that students have completed. They focus on a project from start to finish and show development, problem-solving, and results. Most likely they cover the various levels of thinking and action in Bloom's Taxonomy. They show what a potential employee can do. This is where a teacher's classroom can make the difference by helping the student take the abstract and conceptual and turn it into something tangible, relevant, and meaningful both to the student and to the employers and community.

Assessment

One of the most important responsibilities excellent instructors perform is the assessment of student learning and the effectiveness of their own teaching. According to the 2018 report by the National Academies of Sciences, Engineering, and Math, "Assessment is a critical tool for advancing and monitoring students' learning in school. When grounded in well-defined models of learning, assessment information can be used to identify and subsequently narrow the gap between current and desired levels of students' learning and performance."[45]

Broadly speaking, there are two forms of assessments: formative and summative. Formative is an ongoing assessment which is most likely quick, informal, and often not graded. It consists of a variety of techniques designed to see if students understand the material, or where errors of cognition are being made, before the instructor decides to move forward or to reteach the content. By determining where students' thinking is faulty, the teacher can point out the errors in student understanding, adjust their instruction, and help the learners reconceptualize. Just like the best coaches adapt to their team, the best instructors adapt their instruction to their students' needs.

Summative assessment is most often formal, graded, and summarizes learning at the end of a unit of instruction. Some summative assessments are high stakes. In these cases, a final grade can determine whether a student passes a course or even graduates. Both types of assessment are central to education, but in the estimation of these authors, formative assessment is the most valuable. It is critical to keep in mind that all assessment should be used to provide feedback to the students about their learning and to the instructor about their teaching, not just a formal marking point.

Assessment is an opportunity for the teacher to have a teachable moment—to review the answers after the test is handed back, for example. Everyone who has at one point been a student knows they have guessed the answers to some questions. If the test results are never discussed, students will never know if they guessed correctly, or to have the opportunity to learn the correct answer—they may have just "lucked" into the right answer. This is a missed opportunity for teachers and for learners alike. "The most important function of testing is not to provide a basis for grading. Rather, tests are an important educational tool . . . [for] corrective feedback."[46] The National Academies of Sciences, Engineering, and Medicine elaborated:

> Research suggests that feedback is most effective when it is focused on the task and learning targets; that is, detailed and narrative, not evaluative and graded; delivered in a way that is supportive and aligned with the learner's progress is delivered at a time when the learner can benefit from it; and delivered to a receptive learner who has the self-efficacy needed to respond.[47]

Memory is quite fallible, and people often make mistakes when they attempt to learn new material or to connect it to preexisting knowledge and experience. Metacognitive processes are very helpful in determining where errors may exist.

In addition, low-stakes formative writing exercises help to determine what students know and don't know, and these can provide learners with additional opportunities to think. Such writing prompts help students know what is important and what to explore, process, and learn about. It keeps them focused, gives them practice in writing for later high-stakes assessments, helps them put concepts into their own words, and engages them in their own learning. Formative assessments also indicate to the learners what the instructors deem most important.

The use of high-stakes assessments should be limited. There is frequently a sense by employers that college students can't *do* anything other than take tests. When high-stakes assessment is required, since such high risk is involved, the accuracy of these tests is imperative. Forms of triangulation or multiple measures can help to mitigate some of these concerns. Grading rubrics can help provide validity and reliability. Rubrics can also be useful tools to guide instruction and to help students know what the teacher considers to be important. Often the best instructors will share grading rubrics with the students at the beginning of the learning segment providing the learners with guideposts for success.

Authentic and performance-based assessments are also strategies that can help mitigate concerns of high-stakes tests. Such examples as case studies, scenarios, and real-life and community problems are good examples. Interrater reliability becomes an issue when grading authentic assessments, even when using rubrics for that matter. Practice sessions for instructors are advised. Every seasoned teacher knows that they can grade a paper one day and score it differently another day. This situation is exacerbated if multiple instructors are grading the students' work. In other words, one teacher can grade the same assignments differently in their own classroom, and the assignment scores become unreliable and therefore invalid.

Finally, assessment needs to be purposefully built into the instruction, and it needs to become a part of our instructional routine. It needs to measure the quality of the students' learning and cognition. The old saw, "What gets assessed gets learned," could not be truer. For students preparing for exams, "cramming" is not effective. The brain needs time to process and to make connections. "The best way to prepare for a final exam is to mentally review the material periodically during the day, until the memory becomes part of your long-term memory."[48]

Still, not everything we teach or that the students do needs to be assessed or given a grade. Quite frankly, some things are just very difficult to assess and to measure. McKeachie and Svinicki bemoaned, "Admittedly, it is more difficult to devise measures of complex, higher-level objectives."[49] A quick review of Bloom's Learning Taxonomy is warranted again (figure 3.3). Lower-level learning objectives on Bloom's Taxonomy are typically easy to measure with factual kinds of examinations. The further one goes up the taxonomy, however, the more difficult it is to measure and to be valid in the assessment. Instructors need to be careful when assigning grades and other high-stakes decisions based on ever-increasing concerns of measurement validity.

We conclude now with examples of curriculum mapping, teaching strategies, assignments, and assessments in the teaching approaches of behaviorism, cognitivism, and constructivism. Teachers in each content area will of course adapt these for their own content areas, to their own preferences, and to their students' needs. Further adjustments would need to be made, of course, depending whether teaching is done in-person or online.

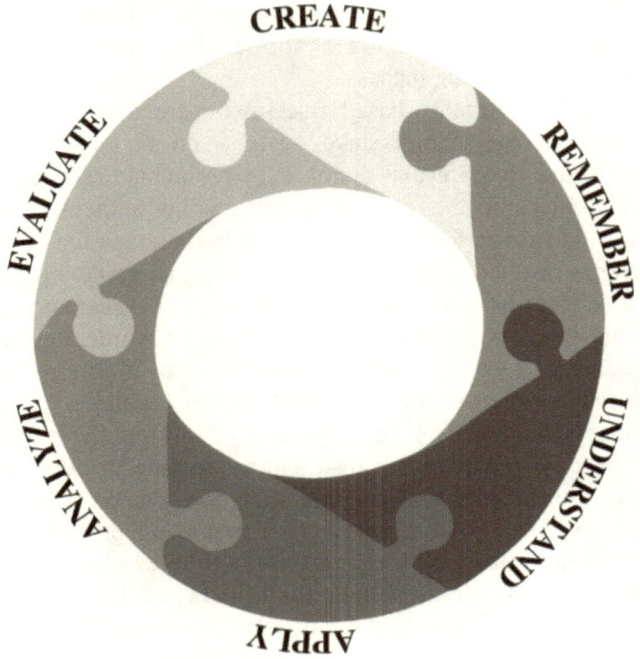

Figure 3.3 Bloom's Learning Taxonomy

THE CASE METHOD

Gorski and Pothini[50] explained that the case method is one powerful tool for enhancing our ability to interpret how students learn. The case method involves analyzing real-life scenarios based on actual events, allowing us to apply theoretical ideas, such as nature versus nurture, to professional practice. By engaging in the case method, we can actively practice navigating through a process that involves considering various angles and perspectives in social interactions. It enables us to explore the intricate complexities of school and classroom situations and, as a result, helps us develop a more intentional approach to educating our students.

Different from traditional approaches, the case method does not provide a single correct answer or an obvious solution. Instead, it mirrors the nature of the real world, where answers are elusive and solutions are subject to debate and contestation. "The case method has us muddle through the gray areas by considering all that makes them gray."[51] It fosters critical thinking abilities, problem-solving skills, and other competencies that are essential for navigating complex educational contexts.

As you read the case studies in this section of the book, use figure 3.4 to help you interpret the cases and draw reflections about how students learn.

CASE ANALYSIS:

Figure 3.4 Case Analysis
Source: Modified version created by Dr. Toni Bailey from the Gorski & Pothini's Figure 2.1 (2018)

In each case, as you move through these steps, consider all sides involved, the influences of the environment, and how students' learning capacities are affected. Diagnose and consider the perspectives, where things went wrong if they did, and what you might have done differently.

THE CASE STUDIES

What Knowledge Is Worth Knowing?

- Case 1 - Last Night's Dinner
- Case 2 - Life Is Not Fair
- Case 3 - I'm Not *Smart* Smart
- Case 4 - Old Fashioned

Nature versus Nurture

- Case 5 - My Little Basketball Player
- Case 6 - Photosynthesis
- Case 7 - Field Trip
- Case 8 - What Did You Call Me!?

Foundational Learning Theories

- Case 9 - Genius Hour
- Case 10 - I Am Going to Count Down from Five
- Case 11 - Dress Nicely
- Case 12 - Giving In

WHAT KNOWLEDGE IS WORTH KNOWING?

Case 1 - Last Night's Dinner

"Class settle down, settle down," Mrs. Hardy said as her third-grade students walked into the classroom at the beginning of the school day. Minutes later, the class became silent, and Mrs. Hardy began to teach them. Her first lesson of the day was a science lesson. Mrs. Hardy said, "Okay everyone, let's continue the science discussion that we had yesterday. We were discussing the importance of eating healthy meals. Danita, tell us about a healthy meal that you ate last night and how it helped your body."

Danita confidently said, "My momma made us some broccoli, chicken, and rice. She always be cooking good! And . . . "

Before Danita could finish, Mrs. Hardy said, "Danita, don't speak like that, it's unprofessional. If you want people to take you seriously you cannot say things like *she always be cooking*. Leave that at-home talk *at* your home. Okay, now go on, tell us how your dinner helped your body."

Danita nervously continued, but now speaking at a much lower volume. After she finished speaking, she sat down in her chair and looked out the window as Mrs. Hardy called on the next student.

Reflection Questions:

1. Why might language variations exist among citizens living in the same region?
2. From your experience, what is the dominant norm for language in schools or general business environments in the United States?
3. What types of labels are associated with different English language variations?
4. Address the assumptions made by the teacher in this case study. How do the assumptions relate to Danita's intellect?

WHAT KNOWLEDGE IS WORTH KNOWING?

Case 2 - Life Is Not Fair

"Man, you just don't get it! You have no idea what you are talking about!" Jermaine continued yelling at a student. "The news is lying, they are not telling the whole story about what's going on in Côte d'Ivoire!"

"Jermaine, Jermaine," Mr. Walker rushed into the classroom. "I could hear you shouting in the hallway, what is going on?

Jermaine replied to Mr. Walker, "I am just getting tired of the news and the absence of all perspectives, but I know that you would not understand."

Mr. Walker responded, "I seriously doubt they would neglect to speak on different perspectives regarding what is going on in the world. Besides, it doesn't really matter because it has nothing to do with what is going on in this classroom."

Jermaine responded, "But I'm from there, and they are trying to make it seem like my people are unfairly putting children into labor in the cocoa fields but they are not providing the whole story. They are making it seem bad, but us working in the cocoa fields from an early age comes with many good life skills."

Mr. Walker replied, "Well look, life is unfair, you have to just ignore it and not get upset. No need to get emotional about it."

Reflection Questions:

1. Neurologically, how is Jermaine affected by what his classmates and the news are saying?
2. What environment has Mr. Walker created in his response to Jermaine's complaint?
3. Is this conflict meaningful to Jermaine's academic growth? Explain.

WHAT KNOWLEDGE IS WORTH KNOWING?

Case 3 - I'm Not *Smart* Smart

Dear Diary,

> All my friends are so good in math class. They do not ever seem to make mistakes. It's like they were just naturally born knowing how to do math or something. Man, I wish that I was naturally born knowing math. Then, I would be the smartest kid in school, and I could do anything. But I wasn't born with it. I mean, I'm smart in language arts and social studies. But I'm not smart smart, because I stink in math. And I'm so scared to speak up in class to ask questions because then, everyone would definitely know that I stink in it.

Reflection Questions:

1. How does this student perceive smartness?
2. What potential environmental influences may have led this student to value math skills the way they do?
3. Are skills innate, or can they be acquired? Explain.
4. How does the fear of failure affect this student's academic integrity, and how might they overcome it?

WHAT KNOWLEDGE IS WORTH KNOWING?

Case 4 - Old Fashioned

"You all are interested in the silliest things. You make videos of yourselves dancing, your music interests are horrible, and you want everything to happen right away. You know, I'm kind of concerned about our future."

Sarah stated, "Well, we like these things, so, I mean, what is the big deal!?"

Her mom responded, "Your priorities are just out of whack; that is the big deal! When I was growing up, we did not have cellular phones or the internet, so we spent most of our time outside with the neighborhood kids. Our music was about unity and peace, and we just took our time with things. I wish that things were still the same. You all have no idea what you are missing. Hopefully, the new principal at your school will rewind the clock and bring things back to how they used to be. Old-fashioned discipline and out with the technology!"

Reflection Questions:

1. What is your perspective of this parent's view of the "way things used to be"?
2. How does time shift cultural norms?
3. How can generational gaps create misunderstandings and the marginalization of what people know?
4. Why do our brains dispel change?
5. What are the advantages and disadvantages of social progression?

NATURE VERSUS NURTURE

Case 5 - My Little Basketball Player

"Hey, little Scottie. You are just the cutest baby that I have ever seen! I love you so so much! I love your little eyes, your cute little ears, and your sweet little baby nose! And look at those long legs! For a two-year-old you sure are tall, and you know what, it's because your dad is pretty tall too! And guess what? He is a basketball player. Isn't that cool!?"

"I think that you will be a basketball player just like him . . . because you like to run and jump! Come on, let's go outside and play basketball. Do you want to do that? Okay, let's go!"

"All right, little Scottie, here is the basketball, your favorite toy that we play with every day, and your dad loves it too! Go ahead, try to shoot it in the hoop. You can do it. I know you can. You are just like your dad. Go, Scottie, go!"

"You did it! You shot it in the hoop! Great work! Can you do it again!? . . . Oh, great job, you did it again! I can't wait to tell your dad when he gets home."

Three hours later . . . with little Scottie in earshot, "Hey Scott, guess what little Scottie did today?! He shot the basketball in the hoop three times! Can you believe that? I think that he's got the genes!"

Reflection Questions:

1. How does the nurture provided to little Scottie potentially influence his nature?
2. Considering this scenario, what might little Scottie consider ideal and necessary at two years old?
3. If this type of nurture continues, what skills might Scottie learn? Why would he learn them?

NATURE VERSUS NURTURE

Case 6 - Photosynthesis

"Okay, everybody, take out your textbooks and turn to page fifty-seven. Today, we will go over photosynthesis," Mr. Green announced to the class.

"Ah geesh, I hate this stuff," Jeff mumbled.

"What was that, Jeff?" Mr. Green asked.

"Nothing," said Jeff, looking miserable.

"Look, everyone, I don't know how many times I have to say this . . . if you don't like science, that's tough. But you need to take this class. Some of us are going places and are good at science. Some of us are simply not going anywhere. It's your choice; you can do it, but I am not going to stand here and beg those of us who don't care," Mr. Green stated firmly.

"Anyways, as I was saying, turn to page fifty-seven. Now I am going to read the chapter to you, listen quietly and pay attention. If you are unable to sit quietly and listen as I read, then hey, like I said earlier, you just may not be good at this subject because your brain is choosing not to be," Mr. Green said.

Reflection Questions:

1. How does this classroom environment influence Jeff's motivation to engage?
2. What are the implications of this classroom environment and Jeff's future?

NATURE VERSUS NURTURE

Case 7 - Field Trip!

Mrs. Jackson announced to the class, "Before we go on the field trip to the city zoo, make sure you find your buddy that I have paired you up with, sit with them on the bus, and stay with them during the zoo tour."

Devontae found his partner and nervously said, "Hi Shane. I guess we are partners. Are you excited about the field trip?"

"Ummm, not really," said Shane.

"Why not?" asked Devontae.

"Because my dads are zoologists, and we go on trips to visit and study animals in their natural habitats all the time."

"Oh, yeah, well, that makes sense," Devontae responded. "Maybe you will still have fun anyway."

Once they arrived at the zoo, Shane and Devontae followed the tour guide, and Shane commented on each animal that they visited with expertise and excitement. "Hey Shane, you are pretty smart with this animal stuff, and pretty cool too. What else do you like to do? Honestly, I barely know anything about you," Devontae said.

Back at school, the students were asked to detail what they learned from the field trip. Mrs. Jackson gave each student an opportunity to contribute to the discussion. When it was Shane's turn, he responded with excitement that he really enjoyed having a great deal of background knowledge on the animals that they visited.

Mrs. Jackson then responded, "Shane, we have been in school for six months and have covered the animal kingdom in class, but I had no idea that you knew so much about animals. How do you know so much?"

Shane responded, "Well, my dads are zoologists, and we go on trips to study animals a lot, and I learn a lot."

Then another student commented: "What I learned most about the zoo was about my partner Veronica. I did not even know her name before today."

Reflection Questions:

1. What environment has the teacher created among her students and the classroom?
2. How do the students engage with each other during the field trip?
3. How might the relationships among the students influence their ability to learn?

Implications and Applications 97

NATURE VERSUS NURTURE

Case 8 - What Did You Call Me!?

"Now that you all have gotten settled into your continued pop art paintings, I'm going to come to take a peek to see how each of you is doing," said Jay, the teacher.

Jay walked around the room, assessing each student's progress and making sure to give relevant, supportive, and targeted feedback. "Oh, fantastic work, Dominique. Your monochromatic color schemes complement each other well. Someone has definitely been using the color wheel to make their color choices!"

"Junior, great craftsmanship with your brush strokes. I find it helpful to add a little extra water to the brush to keep the paint marks smooth."

Then Jay moved over to Jasmine's painting. It was, without a doubt, spectacular work. Jay commented, "Jasmine, that is a very strong painting that you are working on. It's excellent. You are an excellent painter, and I love the subject matter that you've chosen!"

"What did you call me!" Jasmine snapped.

Jay responded, confused, "I said that you were an excellent painter."

"Don't call me that," Jasmine said angrily and with a slightly raised volume.

"What do you mean? You are excellent," Jay responded.

"I am not excellent! Don't call me that word!" Jasmine said, even more angrily than her last response.

Jay repeated, "You are excellent, Jasmine." Jay was so confused, taken aback, slightly offended, and wondered how this encounter had gone so wrong so fast. Why was Jasmine so upset? *She was pretty nice every other day*, Jay thought.

Reflection Questions:

1. How could Jasmine's past "nurture" experiences affect her reaction to Jay?
2. What is happening to them neurologically when students respond with that degree of anger as Jasmine did?
3. What can teachers or parents do to de-escalate such situations?
4. Should Jay have been offended? Why or why not?

FOUNDATIONAL LEARNING THEORIES

Case 9 - Genius Hour

"So, for this assignment, you all are investigating your individual interests. Today, we will brainstorm what we are interested in and what we want to know more about, and then we will start to think about how we can find solutions that can help better our interests. This project is called the 'Genius Hour,' a concept created by Google. Basically, we will spend the next couple of months becoming experts in topics that are uniquely important to each of us. It is my hope that this project influences you to think deeper about what you care about and potentially how it can help guide your future career decisions . . . just maybe . . . or at least the very least to have fun exploring!" Mr. Blake announced to the class.

"Wait, what do you mean, we can do our projects on things that we are interested in and want to know more about? Can we work with partners if we want to?" said a student.

Mr. Blake responded, "Yes, exactly. Today, I want you to brainstorm your project ideas. You will start by developing a question about a topic . . . something that you are curious about and want to know more about. Then, you will research the topic to find out more about it and eventually develop a method to improve it. At the end of this project, we will present our work to the class."

He continued, "So think big! Assume that you are already in a career role, such as an author, video game creator, piano teacher, instructional film producer, cupcake artist, rocket designer, architect, sports illustrator, website designer, visual-social activist, or historian. How can you explore an issue related to your career? After you've finished working on your research, I want you not just to stand here and talk to your classmates about it but to create something original to represent what you found and your ideas. So, start to think about your final project, which could take the form of things like short instructional videos, websites, public service campaigns, how-to books, graphic novels, presentations of paintings, drawings, photographs, rocket models, and online video games."

Reflection Questions:

1. How is this teacher engaging the students?
2. How might what the students create influence their cognition?
3. Describe the rigor involved in the proposed Genius Hour and if you believe students can direct their learning.

4. What are some potential ways of making this learning scenario more effective?

FOUNDATIONAL LEARNING THEORIES

Case 10 - I Am Going to Count Down from Five

"Alrighty, class, let's get seated and ready to work," Mrs. Johnson announced. "I am going to count down from five, and when I reach zero, I need you to be in your seats and brains ready to learn. And there is a special reward for those that do so. Okay, five . . . four . . . three . . . two . . . one . . . zero."

"Jackie, Jenny, and Zach, why are you not in your seats?" Mrs. Johnson asked.

"I could not sit down because I smelled something funny," Jackie said.

"I could not sit down and get ready to learn because I noticed that it was raining outside," Jenny commented.

"And I could not sit down because, well, I just did not want to," Zach chimed in.

"Oh, I see. Well, that makes sense. I will go ahead and give you all the special rewards anyway because I know that you are trying your best. The special reward is five scholar dollars!" Mrs. Johnson responded.

"If Jackie, Jenny, and Zach are getting rewarded for not sitting down, why am I sitting down? I'm confused," Billy said to himself.

Reflection Questions:

1. How do patterns affect how students learn?
2. Is there a connection between what one says and what one does?

FOUNDATIONAL LEARNING THEORIES

Case 11 - Dress Nicely

"Jack, are you ready for school?" Jack's mom shouted from downstairs in the kitchen.

"Yes, mom, almost," Jack replied.

"Make sure that you wear something nice today. You have your award ceremony."

Jack was adopted two years ago and really loves his adoptive parents. They always support and care for him. He had thought to himself all morning about what would look nice for his award ceremony and was so proud to receive his honors. And now that he was ready, he headed downstairs.

"Uh Jack, what is that? I asked you to put on something nice," Jack's mom said.

"But this is . . . nice," Jack said, confused.

"Jack, a jersey and some khaki pants are not nice. I know that you have nice clothes upstairs in your closet. Put on something, you know, professional," said Jack's mom.

Jack thought to himself, *But I thought that this was pretty nice. It's what I used to see people wear to special events. I don't get it.*

"But Mom, why isn't what I have on nice?"

Reflection Questions:

1. What caused the miscommunication in this case?
2. How might Jack's previous experiences have affected his definition of *nice*?
3. In terms of culture, is there one prescribed definition of *nice*? Why or why not?
4. What other miscommunications have you encountered because of different cultural values?

FOUNDATIONAL LEARNING THEORIES

Case 12 - Giving In

"I . . . WANT . . . THE . . . DOLL! Waahhhh!" Cindy cried. Moreover, as she cried, she peeked between her fingers, covering her face to see if anyone was looking, momentarily pausing her crying. Her dad ignored her, looking out of the window. He had offered to give Cindy her doll just a few minutes ago, and she refused it. So he put it in her toy box, and her reaction was to scream and cry.

"I . . . WANT . . . THE . . . DOLL!" Cindy screamed again. "Wahhhhh," and then she peeked between her hands, covering her face again to see if her dad was going to turn around.

"Okay, okay, Cindy," said Cindy's dad after she had cried and screamed for about two minutes. "Here is your doll. I will take it back out of the toy chest."

Reflection Questions:

1. When considering the concept of conditioning, who is conditioning who here?
2. If the father's response continues to similar actions that Cindy does in the future, what might she learn?

3. What may have been Cindy's motivation for her behavior?
4. How would you have responded to Cindy?

NOTES

1. John Bransford, Ann Brown, and Rodney Cocking, eds., *How People Learn: Brain, Mind, Experience, and School* (Washington, DC: National Academy Press, 2000), 155–56.

2. Robert Sylwester, *A Celebration of Neurons: An Educator's Guide to the Human Brain* (Alexandria, VA: Association for Supervision and Curriculum Development, 1995), 23–24.

3. National Academies of Sciences, Engineering, and Medicine, *How People Learn II: Learners, Contexts, and Cultures* (Washington, DC: The National Academies Press, 2018), 6, citing the work of Draganski et al. and Lovden et al., National Academies wrote: "This research emphasizes that a core mechanism of learning—the brain's ability to modify its connections on the basis of new experiences—functions effectively throughout the life span." Bogdan Draganski, Christian Gaser, Volker Busch, Gerhard Schuirer, Ulrich Bogdahn, and Arne May, "Neuroplasticity: Changes in Grey Matter Induced by Training," *Nature* 427, no. 6972 (2004): 311–12; Martin Lovden, Nils Bodammer, Simon Kuhn, Jorn Kaufmann, Hartmut Schutze, Claus Tempelmann, Hans-Yochen Heinze, Emrah Duzerl, Florian Schmiedek, and Ulman Lindenberger, "Experience-Dependent Plasticity of White-Matter Microstructure Extends into Old Age," *Neuropsychologia* 48, no. 13 (2010): 3878–83.

4. Eric Jensen and Liesl McConchie, *Brain-Based Learning: Teaching the Way Students Really Learn* (Thousand Oaks, CA: Corwin, 2020), 87. Here, the authors make special note about "coherent construction. . . . Our brains are constructing our new learning. That suggests we are mindful in the process. But unless what we piece together . . . has some meaning, it is not likely to make sense, be valuable, or be recalled" (87).

5. Jane Healy, *Your Child's Growing Mind: Brain Development and Learning from Birth to Adolescence* (New York: Broadway Books, 2007), 217.

6. Ken Bain, *What the Best College Teachers Do* (Cambridge, MA: Harvard University Press, 2004), 18.

7. Sylwester, *A Celebration of Neurons*, 72. Sylwester went on to caution: "By separating emotion from logic and reason in the classroom, we've simplified school management and evaluation, but we've also then separated two sides of one coin—and lost something important in the process. It's impossible to separate emotion from the important activities of life" (75).

8. Laurie Materna, *Jump Start the Adult Learner: How to Engage and Motivate Adults Using Brain-Compatible Strategies* (Thousand Oaks, CA: Corwin Press, 2007), 10. Materna added that the best instruction provides challenging activities. But even more important is the fact that when learning is pleasant, the material is more likely to move into long-term memory, while negative experiences force the middle

brain which is responsible for emotion to downshift to the primitive parts of the brain responsible for fight or flight.

9. Jensen and McConchie, *Brain-Based Learning*, 128.

10. Paulo Freire, *Pedagogy of the Oppressed* (New York: Continuum International Publishing, 1970).

11. Healy, *Your Child's Growing Mind*, 243.

12. National Academies, *How People Learn II*, 117. Here, the Academies cited the research by

Erika Patall, Harris Cooper, and Susan Wynn, "The Effectiveness and Relative Importance of Choice in the Classroom," *Journal of Educational Psychology* 102, no. 4 (2010): 896–915. The Academies elaborated: "Self-determination theory posits that behavior is strongly influenced by three universal, innate, psychological needs—autonomy (the urge to control one's own life), competence (the urge to experience mastery), and psychological relatedness (the urge to interact with, be connected to, and care for others)" (115).

13. Bransford, Brown, and Cocking, *How People Learn*, 61.

14. Jensen and McConchie, *Brain-Based Learning*, 138–40.

15. Abraham Maslow, "A Theory of Human Motivation," *Psychological Review* 50, no. 4 (July 1943): 370–96.

16. Sofie Loyens, Joshua Magda, and Remy Rikers, "Self-Directed Learning in Problem-Based Learning and its Relationships with Self-Regulated Learning," *Educational Psychology Review* 20, no. 4 (2008): 411–27.

17. Erika Patall, "Constructing Motivation Through Choice, Interest, and Interestingness," *Journal of Educational Psychology* 105, no. 2 (2013): 522–34.

18. Healy, *Your Child's Growing Mind*, 346. Healy expressed: "Creating an atmosphere in which *wrong answers* are viewed as a learning opportunity and where [students] are encouraged to take *intellectual risks* may be the most important factor of all" (346).

19. Healy, *Your Child's Growing Mind*, 24.

20. Healy, *Your Child's Growing Mind*, 79. She stated: "Have faith—in childhood and yourself. Children's brains generally seek what they need, and nature has given you the instincts to help them get it." Healy then concluded: "Don't crush children's imagination with overscheduling, excess pressure for achievement, too much stimulation from outside, or insufficient time to play—both physically and mentally" (373).

21. Bransford, Brown, and Cocking, *How People Learn*, 124.

22. Materna, *Jump Start the Adult-Learner*, 28; Robert Leamnson, *Thinking about Teaching and Learning: Developing Habits of Learning with First Year College and University Students* (Sterling, VA: Sylus Publishing, 1999), 13, extended this reasoning: "There are two points of significance here for teachers. First, it is the multiple connections between neurons that allow perceptions and thought. . . . Second, it is experience and sensory interaction with the environment that promotes and stabilizes neural connections."

23. Suzanne Wade, William Buxton, and Michelle Kelly, "Using Think-Alouds to Examine Reader–Text Interest," *Reading Research Quarterly* 34, no. 2 (1999): 194–216, in National Academies, *How People Learn II*, 114.

24. Leamnson, *Thinking about Teaching and Learning*, 78, 81.

25. Richard Restak, *The New Brain: How the Modern Age is Rewiring Your Brain* (Emmaus, PA: Rodale Press, 2003), 21.

26. Colin Rose, *Accelerated Learning Action Guide* (Aylesbury, Buckinghamshire, UK: Accelerated Learning Systems, 1995), in Materna, *Jump Start the Adult Learner*, 37.

27. Leamnson, *Thinking about Teaching and Learning*, 101.

28. Pam Mueller and Daniel Oppenheimer, "The Pen is Mightier than the Keyboard," *Psychological Science* 25, no. 6 (2014): 1159–68.

29. Bransford, Brown, and Cocking, *How People Learn*, 42.

30. Eleanor Duckworth, *"The Having of Wonderful Ideas" and Other Essays on Teaching and Learning* (New York: Teachers College Press, Columbia University, 1987), in Bransford, Brown, and Cocking, *How People Learn*, 136.

Overall, learner-centered environments include teachers who are aware that learners construct their own meanings, beginning with the beliefs, understandings, and cultural practices they bring to the classroom. If teaching is conceived as constructing a bridge between the subject matter and the student, learner-centered teachers keep a constant eye on both ends of the bridge. The teachers attempt to get a sense of what students know and can do as well as their interests and passions—what each student knows, cares about, is able to do, and wants to do. (136)

31. National Academies, *How People Learn II*, 7.

32. Bransford, Brown, and Cocking, *How People Learn*, 136. They elaborated: "[k]nowledge-centered environments also include an emphasis on sense-making—on helping students become metacognitive by expecting new information to make sense and asking clarification when it doesn't" (137).

33. Bransford, Brown, and Cocking, *How People Learn*, 139.

34. Michio Kaku, *The Future of the Mind: The Scientific Quest to Understand, Enhance, and Empower the Mind* (New York: Doubleday, 2014), 51. Kaku elaborated: "It seems that the one characteristic most closely associated with success in life, which has persisted over the decades, is the ability to delay gratification" (137). In citing the work of other researchers, he added to the list: a person's ability to cooperate, regulate emotions, focus attention, motivation, and persistence.

35. Healy, *Your Child's Growing Mind*, 351–52. Healy went on to state: "One large study found that 70 percent of highly creative students were not identified as 'gifted' by IQ scores" (352).

36. Healy, *Your Child's Growing Mind*, 370.

37. Bransford, Brown, and Cocking, *How People Learn*, 139.

38. Stephen Covey, *Seven Habits of Highly Effective People* (New York: Free Press, 1989).

39. Wilbert McKeachie and Marilla Svinicki, *Teaching Tips: Strategies, Research, and Theory for College and University Teachers* (Boston: Houghton-Mifflin, 2006), 36. These authors add: "In lectures . . . research shows that most of the material covered does not make it into students' notes or memory. . . . [and] that, in discussion, students pay attention and think more actively" (36). The authors conclude:

Now we think of knowledge as being stored in structures such as networks with linked concepts, facts, and principles. The lecture thus needs to build a bridge between what is in the students' minds and the structures in the subject matter. Metaphors, examples, and demonstrations are the elements of that bridge. . . . [Now] a typical lecture strives to present a systematic, concise summary of the knowledge to be covered in the day's assignment. . . . Now more of my lectures involve analyzing materials, formulating problems, developing hypotheses, bringing evidence to bear, criticizing and evaluating alternative solutions—revealing methods of learning and thinking and involving students in the process. (60)

40. Leamnson, *Thinking about Teaching and Learning*, 145–46.

41. Terry Flowerday, Gregory Schraw, and Joseph Stevens, "The Role of Choice and Interest in Reader Engagement," *The Journal of Experimental Education* 72, no. 2 (2004): 93–114.

42. Gregory Schraw and Stephen Lehman, "Situational Interest: A Review of the Literature and Directions for Future Research," *Educational Psychology Review* 13, no. 1 (2001): 23–52.

43. National Academies, *How People Learn II*, 114.

44. Barbara Condliffe, Mary Visher, Michael Bangser Sonia Drohojowska, and Larissa Saco, "Project-based Learning: A Literature Review," mdrc Working Paper (2016), https://www.mdrc.org/sites/default/files/Project-Based_Learning-LitRev_Final.pdf.

45. National Academies, *How People Learn II*, 7.

46. McKeachie and Svinicki, *Teaching Tips*, 109.

47. National Academies, *How People Learn II*, 155.

48. Kaku, *The Future of the Mind*, 119.

49. McKeachie and Svinicki, *Teaching Tips*, 77.

50. Paul C. Gorski and Seema G. Pothini, *Case Studies on Diversity and Social Justice Education*, second edition (London: Routledge, 2018).

51. Gorski and Pothini, *Case Studies on Diversity and Social Justice Education*, 7.

Annotated Bibliography

While dozens of books and articles were central to the writing of this book, the following played a significant role and should be considered for any school's professional library or parent's personal library.

Bransford, John, Ann Brown, and Rodney Cocking, eds. *How People Learn: Brain, Mind, Experience, and School.* Washington, DC: National Academies Press, 2000.

> This book is exceptionally well written and focuses exclusively on learning theory and implications for the K–12 classroom. It is thorough and detailed, yet it gives direct implications primarily for the K–12 setting. Like other such books, however, the implications and applications are relevant for instructors at any level. It is written by professional educators for professional educators.

Breslaw, Elaine. "Behaviorism in the Classroom." *Change: The Magazine of Higher Learning*, 5, no. 3 (1973): 52–55.

> This article provides a rare account of how behaviorism can be directly applied to a college or university classroom. Its application is unique though not only because of its rarity but because it emphasizes the idea that behaviorism is not just a strict and mundane perspective of how we learn—it is essentially the basis of rhythmic and scheduled patterns that occur in so many aspects of our everyday lives, and to a great degree are appreciated.

Bueno, David. "Genetics and Learning: How the Genes Influence Educational Attainment." *Frontiers in Psychology* 10 (2019): 1–10.

> This article provides a comprehensive explanation of how educators can influence their students' biological functions through the classroom environment that they establish. Scientific evidence is provided to conclude that genetic traits have been traced to environmental influences. Therefore, the ability to reason or create can be relatively correlated with the degree to which an educator has structured their classroom environment to nurture and optimize those abilities.

Churches, Richard, Eleanor Dommett, and Ian Devonshire. *Neuroscience for Teachers: Applying Research Evidence from Brain Science*. Rocky Hill, CT: Crown House Publishing, 2017.

These authors share contemporary findings in brain research from the perspective of research primarily conducted in the United Kingdom. Thus, there are citations that are not always found in the mainstream of American literature. Still, the reader will find a great deal of overlap in the works across both continents. This is a good introductory read for both parents and teachers alike.

Gardner, Howard. *Frames of Mind: The Theory of Multiple Intelligences*. New York: Basic Books, 1983.

The idea that students learn contingent upon specific learning modalities has been a bit of a point of contention in the field of education. This text provides a convincing argument that our concept of intelligence is contingent upon societal norms. However, if we broaden our scope, we can instead view intelligence as a system of codes or languages that can be transferrable to most learners when they are aware that different learning modalities exist and are taught in a variety of ways that align with them.

Gutek, Gerald. *Historical and Philosophical Foundations of Education: A Biographical Introduction*. New York: Pearson, 2011.

This text provides a comprehensive account of curriculum, from its earliest beginnings to modern day practices. With roughly twenty-five hundred years of curriculum theories, Gutek gives a thorough understanding of each curricular movement and the societal contexts that invoked those movements.

Hammond, Zaretta. *Culturally Responsive Teaching and the Brain: Promoting Authentic Engagement and Rigor among Culturally and Linguistically Diverse Students*. Thousand Oaks, CA: Corwin Press, 2015.

This text introduces culturally responsive teaching through a neurological lens. It provides an in-depth yet digestible overview of achievement disparities, functions of the brain, and the critical role that culturally responsive teaching plays in cognitive processes. This text is very useful for all types of educators and could even extend to leadership roles outside of education as well.

Healy, Jane. *Your Child's Growing Mind: Brain Development and Learning from Birth to Adolescence*. New York: Broadway Books, 2007.

This book is an exceptional read for anyone seeking to understand how children learn and how best to teach them. Its primary audience might seem to be parents, but all audiences will find it relevant. If you are looking for an extremely thorough understanding of the brain's growth and development, this is a must-read, and it's written in laymen terms.

Jensen, Eric, and Liesl McConchie. *Brain-Based Learning: Teaching the Way Students Really Learn.* Thousand Oaks, CA: Corwin, 2020.

Eric Jensen has written numerous books about brain research and its implications for K–12 student populations. Each book is equally relevant to broad audiences. This book, in particular, shares numerous examples and insights for teachers to apply brain-compatible approaches to their own classrooms.

Leamnson, Robert. *Thinking about Teaching and Learning: Developing Habits of Learning with First Year College and University Students.* Sterling, VA: Sylus Publishing. 1999.

This is another book that should be housed in every campus's center for teaching and learning. Leamnson provides an erudite examination of how young college students learn with practical application that can be implemented immediately. This is a very thoughtful read and should be part of any center for teaching and learning book study for serious professors.

Ormrod, Jane Ellis, and Brett Jones. *Essentials of Educational Psychology*, fifth edition. New York: Pearson, 2019.

Dr. Rettig and Dr. Bailey have used this book in their undergraduate and graduate courses for learning and cognition. It is thoroughly researched and written for college and graduate students. While it is written to explain K–12 learners, it has general applicability for wider audiences. Certainly, every school of education should have this book in its library.

Schunk, Dale. *Learning Theories: An Educational Perspective.* New York: Pearson, 2012.

This book provides a foundational and historical account of each of the major learning theories. It is an excellent textbook for students majoring in education. However, much of this text can also be applied to learning in the college classroom as well using the theories and examples to make intentional instructional decisions.

Sylwester, Robert. *A Celebration of Neurons: An Educator's Guide to the Human Brain.* Alexandria, VA: Association for Supervision and Curriculum Development, 1995.

While this book is old, the information is accurate and remains as relevant today as it did when it first came out. The Association for Supervision and Curriculum Development is an exceptional organization devoted to teaching and teacher education. This book focuses primarily on the young mind, but it is relevant for the understanding of all learners.

Wexler, Bruce. *Brain and Culture: Neurobiology, Ideology, and Social Change.* Cambridge, MA: The MIT Press, 2008.

This book provides a comprehensive collection of empirical evidence and discussions on how cultural aspects in environments influence the functioning of the brain. Wexler connects nature and nurture experiences to social negotiations when exposed to new environments. Moreover, the constant back-and-forth effects of the brain behaving as a reaction to its environment and the environment reacting to it are explored.

Bibliography

Abeka, Silvance. *Introduction to Higher Education*. Simple Book Publishing, n.d.
Ames, Carole. "Conceptions of Motivation within Competitive and Noncompetitive Goal Structures." In Ralf Schwarzer (ed.). *Self-related Cognitions in Anxiety and Motivation*, 229–45. Hillsdale, NJ: Lawrence Erlbaum Associates, 1986.
Anderson, Lorin, and David Krathwohl (eds.). *A Taxonomy for Learning, Teaching, and Assessing: A Revision of Bloom's Taxonomy of Educational Objectives*. New York: Longman, 2001.
Applefield, James, Richard Huber, and Mahnaz Moallem. "Constructivism in Theory and Practice: Toward a Better Understanding." *High School Journal* 84, no. 2 (2001): 35–53.
Aristotle. *The Basic Works of Aristotle*. Edited by R. McKeon. New York: Modern Library, 2001.
Bain, Ken. *What the Best College Teachers Do*. Cambridge, MA: Harvard University Press, 2004.
Bengtsson, Sara, Zoltan Nagy, Stefan Skare, Lea Forsman, Hans Forssberg, and Fredrik Ullen. "Extensive Piano Practicing Has Regionally Specific Effects on White Matter Development." *Nature Neuroscience* 8, no. 9 (2005): 1148–50.
Benjamin, Aaron, and Jonathan Tullis, J. "What Makes Distributed Practice Effective?" *Cognitive Psychology* 61, no. 3 (2010): 228–47.
Bloom, Benjamin, M. Engelhart, E. Furst, Hill, and W. Krathwohl. Taxonomy of Educational Objectives: The Classification of Educational Goals. New York: David McKay Company, 1956.
Boyer, Ernest. *Scholarship Reconsidered: Priorities of the Professoriate*. Princeton, NJ: Princeton University Press, 1990.
Bransford, John, Ann Brown, and Rodney Cocking, eds. *How People Learn: Brain, Mind, Experience, and School*. Washington, DC: National Academies Press, 2000.
Caine, Renate Nummela, and Geoffrey Caine. "Understanding a Brain-Based Approach to Learning and Teaching." *Educational Leadership. Association for Supervision and Curriculum Development* (1990): 66–70.
Chang, Yongmin. "Reorganization and Plastic Changes of the Human Brain Associated with Skill Learning and Expertise." *Frontiers in Human Neuroscience* 8, no. 35 (2014).

Chen, Ying-Chih. "Epistemic Uncertainty and the Support of Productive Struggle During Scientific Modeling for Knowledge Co-development." *Journal of Research in Science Teaching* 59, 3 (2022): 383–422.

Churches, Richard, Eleanor Dommett, and Ian Devonshire. *Neuroscience for Teachers: Applying Research Evidence from Brain Science*. New York: Crown House Publishing, 2017.

Condliffe, Barbara, Mary Visher, Michael Bangser Sonia Drohojowska, and Larissa Saco. *Projectbased Learning: A Literature Review*. mdrc Working Paper (2016.

Confucius. *The Analects of Confucius: A Philosophical Translation*, translated by Roger T. Ames and Henry Rosemont Jr. New York: Ballantine Books, 1999.

Covey, Stephen. *Seven Habits of Highly Effective People*. New York: Free Press, 1989.

Csikszentmihalyi, Mihalyi. *Flow: The Psychology of Optimal Experience*. New York: Harper Collins, 1990.

Davies, Gail, Max Lam, Sarah Harris, Joey Trampush, Michelle Luciano, and W. David Hill. "Study of 300,486 Individuals Identifies 148 Independent Genetic Loci Influencing General Cognitive Function." *Nature Communications* 9, no. 1 (2018): 1–16.

Draganski, Bogdan, Christian Gaser, Volker Busch, Gerhard Schuirer, Ulrich Bogdahn, and Arne May. "Neuroplasticity: Changes in Grey Matter Induced by Training." *Nature* 427, no. 6972 (2004): 311–12.

Duckworth, Eleanor. *"The Having of Wonderful Ideas" and Other Essays on Teaching and Learning*. New York: Teachers College Press, Columbia University, 1987.

Duncan-Andrade, Jeffrey M.R. "Note to Educators: Hope Required When Growing Roses in Concrete." *Harvard Educational Review* 79, no. 2 (2009).

Ecker, K. H. Ullrich, Briony Swire, and Stephan Lewandowsky. "Correcting Misinformation—A Challenge for Education and Cognitive Science." In *Processing Inaccurate Information: Theoretical and Implied Perspectives from Cognitive Science and the Educational Sciences*, edited by David Rapp and Jason Braasch. Cambridge, MA: The MIT Press, 2014.

Erikson, Erik. "The Problem of Ego Identity." In *Pivotal Papers on Identification*, edited by G.H. Pollock. Madison, CT: International Universities Press, 1959.

Erman, Adolph. *The Literature of the ancient Egyptians: Poems, Narratives, and Manual of Instruction from the Third and Second Millennia B.C.*, translated by Aylward M. Blackman, 299. London: Routledge Revivals, 1927.

Fahim, Tahmer, and Nagoua Zoair, "Education in Ancient Egypt till the End of the Graeco-Roman Period: Some Evidences for Quality." *Journal of Association of Arab Universities for Tourism and Hospitality* 13, no. 3 (2016): 1–16.

Flowerday, Terry, Gregory Schraw, and Joseph Stevens. "The Role of Choice and Interest in Reader Engagement." *The Journal of Experimental Education* 72, no. 2 (2004): 93–114.

Freire, Paulo. *Pedagogy of the Oppressed*. New York: Continuum International Publishing, 1970.

Gardner, Howard. *Multiple Intelligences*. New York: Basic Books, 1993.

Gardner, Howard. *Frames of Mind: The Theory of Multiple Intelligences.* New York: Basic Books, 1983.

Gehlbach, Hunter, Maureen Brinkworth, Aaron King, Laura Hsu, Joseph McIntyre, and Todd Rogers. "Creating Birds of Similar Feathers: Leveraging Similarity to Improve Teacher–Student Relationship and Academic Achievement." *Journal of Educational Psychology* 108, no. 3 (2016): 342–52.

Generals, Donald Jr. "The Architect of Progressive Education: John Dewey or Booker T. Washington." In *National Association of African American Studies & National Association of Hispanic and Latino Studies: 2000 Literature Monograph Series. Proceedings (Education Section) (Houston, TX, February 21-26, 2000).* 2002.

Gholson, Barry, Amy Witherspoon, Brent Morgan, Joshua Brittingham, Robert Coles, Arthur Graesser, Jeremiah Sullins, and Scotty Craig. "Exploring the Deep-Level Reasoning Questions Effect During Vicarious Learning among Eighth to Eleventh Graders in the Domains of Computer Literacy and Newtonian Physics." *Instructional Science* 37, no. 5 (2009): 487–93.

Goleman, Daniel. *Emotional Intelligence.* New York: Bantam, 1997.

Gorski, Paul, and Seema G. Pothini. *Case Studies on Diversity and Social Justice Education,* second edition. London: Routledge, 2018.

Gutek, Gerald. *Historical and Philosophical Foundations of Education: A Biographical Introduction.* New York: Pearson, 2011.

Hacker, Douglas, "Failures to Detect Textual Problems during Reading." In *Processing Inaccurate Information: Theoretical and Implied Perspectives from Cognitive Science and the Educational Sciences,* edited by David Rapp and Jason Braasch, 88. Cambridge, MA: The MIT Press, 2014.

Hammond, Zaretta. *Culturally Responsive Teaching and the Brain: Promoting Authentic Engagement and Rigor among Culturally and Linguistically Diverse Students.* New York: Corwin Press, 2015.

Hastings, Erin, and Robin West. "Goal Orientation and Self-Efficacy in Relation to Memory in Adulthood." *Aging, Neuropsychology, and Cognition* 18, no. 4 (2011): 471–93.

Healy, Jane. *Your Child's Growing Mind: Brain Development and Learning from Birth to Adolescence.* New York: Broadway Books, 2007.

Holecek, Andrew. *Dream Yoga: Illuminating Your Life through Lucid Dreaming and the Tibetan Yogas of Sleep.* Boulder, CO: Sounds True, 2016.

Immordino-Yang, Mary Helen, and Rebecca Gotlieb. "Embodied Brains, Social Minds, Cultural Meaning: Integrating Neuroscientific and Educational Research on Social-Affective Development." *American Educational Research Journal: Centennial Issue* 54, no. 1 (2017): 344S–367S.

Institute of Medicine. *From Neurons to Neighborhoods: The Science of Early Childhood Development.* Washington, DC: National Academies Press, 2000.

Jensen, Eric, and Liesl McConchie. *Brain-Based Learning: Teaching the Way Students Really Learn.* Thousand Oaks, CA: Corwin, 2020.

Jurgens, Judith. "The Teaching of Khety Twice – A New Reading of oBM EA 65597 as a School Exercise." *The Journal of Egyptian Archaeology* 105, no. 1 (2020).

Kaku, Michio. *The Future of the Mind: The Scientific Quest to Understand, Enhance, and Empower the Mind.* New York: Doubleday, 2014.

Leamnson, Robert. *Thinking about Teaching and Learning: Developing Habits of Learning with First Year College and University Students.* Sterling, VA: Sylus Publishing, 1999.

Leisman, Gerry, Raed Mualem, and Safa Khayat Mughrabi. "The Neurological Development of the Child with the Educational Enrichment in Mind." *Psicología Educativa* 21, no. 2 (2015): 79–96.

Lenroot, Rhosel, and Jay Giedd. "Brain Development in Children and Adolescents: Insights from Anatomical Magnetic Resonance Imaging." *Neuroscience Biobehavioral Review* 30, no. 6 (2006): 718–29.

Levitin, Daniel. *This is Your Brain on Music: The Science of a Human Obsession.* New York: Plume of Penguin Group, 2006.

Lovden, Martin, Nils Bodammer, Simon Kuhn, Jorn Kaufmann, Hartmut Schutze, Claus Tempelmann, Hans-Yochen Heinze, Emrah Duzerl, Florian Schmiedek, and Ulman Lindenberger. "Experience-Dependent Plasticity of White-Matter Microstructure Extends into Old Age." *Neuropsychologia* 48, no. 13 (2010): 3878–83.

Loyens, Sofie, Joshua Magda, and Remy Rikers. "Self-Directed Learning in Problem-Based Learning and its Relationships with Self-Regulated Learning." *Educational Psychology Review* 20, no. 4 (2008): 411–27.

Marzano, Robert, and John Kendall. *The New Taxonomy of Educational Objectives.* Thousand Oaks, CA: Corwin Press, 2006.

Maslow, Abraham. "A Theory of Human Motivation." *Psychological Review* 50, no. 4 (July 1943): 370–96.

Materna, Laurie. *Jump Start the Adult Learner: How to Engage and Motivate Adults Using Brain-Compatible Strategies.* Thousand Oaks, CA: Corwin Press, 2007.

McKeachie, Wilbert, and Marilla Svinicki. *Teaching Tips: Strategies, Research, and Theory for College and University Teachers.* Boston: Houghton-Mifflin, 2006.

Medaglia, John, Mary-Ellen Lynall, and Danielle Bassett. "Cognitive Network Neuroscience." *Journal of Cognitive Neuroscience* 27, no. 8 (2015): 1471–91.

MIT Technology Review. *New Measures of Human Brain Processing Speed.* August 25, 2009, https://www.technologyreview.com/2009/08/25/210267/new-measure-of-human-brain-processing-speed/.

Mueller, Pam, and Daniel Oppenheimer. "The Pen is Mightier than the Keyboard." *Psychological Science* 25, no. 6 (2014): 1159–68.

National Academies of Sciences, Engineering, and Medicine. *How People Learn II: Learners, Contexts, and Cultures.* Washington, DC: The National Academies Press, 2018.

National Research Council. *Education for Life and Work: Developing Transferable Knowledge and Skills in the 21st Century.* Washington, DC: The National Academies Press, 2012.

National Research Council and Institute of Medicine. *Transforming the Workforce for Children Birth Through Age 8: A Unifying Foundation.* Washington, DC: The National Academies Press, 2015.

Ormrod, Jane Ellis, and Brett Jones. *Essentials of Educational Psychology.* New York: Pearson, 2019.

Patall, Erika. "Constructing Motivation Through Choice, Interest, and Interestingness." *Journal of Educational Psychology* 105, no. 2 (2013): 522–34.

Patall, Erika, Harris Cooper, and Susan Wynn. "The Effectiveness and Relative Importance of Choice in the Classroom." *Journal of Educational Psychology* 102, no. 4 (2010): 896–915.

Piaget, Jean. *Play, Dreams, and Imitation in Childhood.* New York: Norton & Co., 1962.

Rapp, David, and Jason Braasch (eds). *Processing Inaccurate Information.* Cambridge, MA: MIT Press, 2014.

Restak, Richard. *The New Brain: How the Modern Age is Rewiring Your Brain.* Emmaus, PA: Rodale Press, 2003.

Rose, Colin. *Accelerated Learning Action Guide.* Aylesbury, Buckinghamshire, UK: Accelerated Learning Systems, 1995.

Schraw, Gregory, and Stephen Lehman. "Situational Interest: A Review of the Literature and Directions for Future Research." *Educational Psychology Review* 13, no. 1 (2001): 23–52.

Schunk, Dale. *Learning Theories: An Educational Perspective.* New York, NY: Pearson, 2012.

Schwarzer, Ralf (ed.). *Self-related Cognitions in Anxiety and Motivation.* Hillsdale, NJ: Lawrence Erlbaum Associates, 1986.

Seifert, Colleen. "The Continued Influence Effect: The Persistence of Misinformation in Memory and Reasoning Following Correction." In *Processing Inaccurate Information: Theoretical and Implied Perspectives from Cognitive Science and the Educational Sciences*, edited by David Rapp and Jason Braasch, 39. Cambridge, MA: The MIT Press, 2014.

Shlain, Leonard. *The Alphabet Versus the Goddess: The Conflict Between Word and Image.* New York: Penguin Group, 1998.

Simmons, Roberta G., and Dale A. Blythe. *Moving into Adolescence: The Impact of Pubertal Change and School Context.* New York: Routledge, 1987.

Skinner, B.F. "Whatever Happened to Psychology as the Science of Behavior?" *American Psychologist* 42, no. 8 (1987): 780–86.

Sporns, Olaf. *Networks of the Brain.* Cambridge, MA: MIT Press, 2011.

Sternberg, Robert. *Successful Intelligence.* New York: Plume, 1997.

Sylwester, Robert. *A Celebration of Neurons: An Educator's Guide to the Human Brain.* Alexandria, VA: Association for Supervision and Curriculum Development, 1995.

Talbot, Michael. *The Holographic Universe.* New York: Harper Collins, 1991.

Thompson, Evan. *Waking, Dreaming, Being: Self and Consciousness in Neuroscience, Meditation, and Philosophy.* New York: Columbia University Press, 2017.

Thorndike, Edward. *Animal Intelligence: Experimental Studies.* New York: Macmillan, 1911.

Tolman, Edward. "Instinct and Purpose." *Psychological Review* 27, no. 3 (1920): 217–33.

Vygotsky, Lev. "The Role of Play in Development." In *Mind in Society*, translated by M. Cole, 92–104. Cambridge, MA: Harvard University Press, 1978.

Wade, Suzanne, William Buxton, and Michelle Kelly, Michelle. "Using Think-Alouds to Examine Reader–Text Interest." *Reading Research Quarterly* 34, no. 2 (1999): 194–216.

Washington, Booker T. "Principal's Annual Report." Unpublished manuscript. Tuskegee Institute. BTW Papers, Library of Congress, 1902.

Wexler, Bruce E. *Brain and Culture: Neurobiology, Ideology, and Social Change*. Cambridge, MA: The MIT Press, 2008.

Wiggins, Grant, and Jay McTighe. *Understanding by Design*. Alexandria, VA: Association for Supervision and Curriculum Development, 2005.

Williams, Raymond. *Culture and Society 1780-1950*. London, UK: Chatto and Windus, 1958.

Wolf, Fred Alan. *The Dreaming Universe: A Mind-Expanding Journey into the Realm Where Psyche and Physics Meet*. New York: Touchstone, 1994.

Yilmaz, Kaya. "The Cognitive Perspective on Learning: Its Theoretical Underpinnings and Implications for Classroom Practices." Clearing House: A Journal of Educational Strategies, Issues and Ideas 84, no. 5 (2011): 204–12.

Zakin, Andrea. "Metacognition and the Use of Inner Speech in Children's Thinking: A Tool Teachers Can Use." *Journal of Education and Human Development* 1, no. 2 (2007): 1–14.

About the Authors

Perry R. Rettig, PhD, started his educational career in 1984 as a public school teacher in rural Green Bay, Wisconsin. He taught fourth grade, fifth grade, fourth-/fifth-grade combined class, and seventh-/eighth-grade English and literature over a five-year span. Subsequently, he became a public school principal for seven years in Sheboygan, Wisconsin, serving at both the elementary and middle school levels.

After those initial twelve years in the K–12 setting, Rettig became a professor of educational leadership and administration. His first year of service began at Northern State University in Aberdeen, South Dakota. He then moved back to Wisconsin to serve as a professor of educational leadership and administration at the University of Wisconsin-Oshkosh. While there, he eventually served as chancellor's leadership fellow and then associate vice chancellor for academic affairs.

In 2013 he moved to Piedmont University north of Atlanta, Georgia, where he served as vice president for academic affairs. Over the next years he also served in the roles of vice president of the Athens Campus, vice president for student affairs and enrollment management, and even served in the capacity of interim dean of nursing and health sciences and interim dean of education. In 2022, he returned to the classroom as distinguished university professor, making a full circle of his educational career.

Dr. Rettig received his bachelor's degree in education from the University of Wisconsin-Whitewater, his master's degree in educational leadership from the University of Wisconsin-Milwaukee, and his doctorate degree in educational leadership from Marquette University. This is his eleventh book, tenth with Rowman & Littlefield.

Toni M. Bailey, PhD, began her educational career as a first-grade charter schoolteacher in New Orleans, Louisiana, shortly after Hurricane Katrina devastated the area. After serving a year in that role, she became a middle school art teacher at Druid Hills Middle School in Decatur, Georgia, where she served in that role and as well as the elective department chair for nine years. Following her K–12 experience, she became an assistant professor of education in the department of advanced graduate studies at Piedmont University in Athens, Georgia.

Dr. Bailey received her bachelor's degree in fine arts from Xavier University of Louisiana and her master's degree in the art of teaching and her doctorate degree in curriculum and instruction from Mercer University. Additionally, her research includes learning and cognition as it relates to social and cultural capital.

www.ingramcontent.com/pod-product-compliance
Lightning Source LLC
Chambersburg PA
CBHW030144240426
43672CB00005B/269